Global Perspectives

Reading & Writing Book 1

by

Noriko Nakanishi

Nicholas Musty

Shoko Otake

Tam Shuet Ying

Mary Ellis

音声ファイルのダウンロード／ストリーミング

CD マーク表示がある箇所は、音声を弊社 HP より無料でダウンロード／ストリーミングすることができます。下記 URL の書籍詳細ページに音声ダウンロードアイコンがございますのでそちらから自習用音声としてご活用ください。

https://www.seibido.co.jp/ad688

Global Perspectives
Reading & Writing Book 1

はしがき

インターネットの発達により、日本国内にいても、英文を読み、自分が伝えたいことを発信することができる時代になりました。また、自分で英文を読んだり書いたりしなくても、大まかな内容ならば日本語に翻訳されたものを読み、日本語で書いた文を英語に自動翻訳する技術はすでに一般的になっています。しかし、単に概要を把握したり伝えたりするだけでなく、相手の真意を読み取り、分かりやすく伝えるためには、文のニュアンスを読み取って論点を整理し、相手の文化や考え方の背景を尊重しながら自分の考えを自分の言葉で順序よく伝える必要があります。

さらに、同じ内容を伝えようとする英文であっても、E メール文、ブログ、チャット、張り紙、パンフレットのように日常的に目にする英文にはそれぞれ特徴的な書き方がありますし、学術的なエッセイや論文には、決まったスタイルがあります。一方、英文を機械翻訳で和訳したものを読み、日本語で作文したものを機械翻訳で英訳していると、途中どこかのプロセスで誤訳や場面にふさわしくない表現が紛れ込む危険性がつきまといます。場面や状況に応じて文章を効率よく読み、書き分けるコミュニケーション力が、今後の社会では一層求められます。

本書のねらいは、学習者が大学入学までに培ってきた以下の「三つの柱（文部科学省、2018年3月公示）」を引き継ぎ、さらに発展させることです。

(1) 何を理解しているか、何ができるか（知識・技能）
(2) 理解していること・できることをどう使うか（思考力・判断力・表現力）
(3) どのように社会・世界と関わり、よりよい人生を送るか（学びに向かう力・人間性）

本書の Book 1 では大学生が日常的に経験する「大学生活」「心と体の健康」のようなトピック、Book 2 では「学術研究」「科学とは」のような、大学生にふさわしい学際的なトピックを扱います。ユニットごとのトピックに関連するパッセージを読んでリーディング力を養うだけでなく、情報を整理し、多様な角度から検討した上で、論理的・客観的に自分の意見を述べるための批判的思考力をつけることを目的としています。近年の社会情勢を反映させた話題や、賛否が分かれることがらを取り上げたパッセージを読んだうえで、自分の意見を整理して英語で述べるためのライティングアウトラインの作成へとつなげます。本書を通して、学習者が英語のリーディング力やライティング力を伸ばすだけでなく、思考力・判断力・表現力や積極性・人間性を養うきっかけとなることを願っています。

最後に、本書の出版にあたり、趣旨をご理解くださり、きめ細やかなアドバイスでサポートくださった（株）成美堂編集部の中澤ひろ子氏に、心から感謝を申し上げます。

2023 年 11 月
筆者一同

本書の構成 / 使い方

❶ Warm-up

　各ユニットに関連したトピックについて 4 つの選択肢の中から自分の知識や考えに近いものを選び、ウォーミングアップをしましょう。時間に余裕があれば、なぜその選択肢を選んだか説明し、クラスメイトと意見交換しましょう。

❷ Words in Focus

　各ユニットに関連した用語を予め確認しましょう。単に英単語を和訳するのではなく、用語をネット検索して、トピックと関連する背景知識を身につけておきましょう。

❸ Casual Reading

　ホームページやメール、ブログ、チャット、張り紙、パンフレットような日常的に目にする短いパッセージを読みましょう。パッセージ内の 3 か所は穴埋め問題になっています。前後の文脈を読み取ってふさわしい語句を選択しましょう。続いて、内容確認問題が 3 問あります。そのうちの 1 つは、パッセージに加えて、スマホ画面やシンボル、広告、図表のような情報も参考にして回答する問題です。TOEIC Part 7 ダブルパッセージ問題の練習としても活用することができます。

❹ Reading Tips

　上記の短いパッセージの要点をまとめた穴埋め問題に回答し、パッセージを読む際のコツをつかみましょう。以下は、各ユニットで紹介されるリーディングのコツです。

Unit	コツ	Unit	コツ
1	Main idea and details (1)	7	Sequencing
2	Dealing with unknown words	8	Comparison and contrast
3	Cause and effect	9	Main idea and details (2)
4	Understanding timelines	10	Inference (1)
5	Similarities and differences	11	Inference (2)
6	Categorizing	12	Paraphrasing

❺ Academic Reading

　Book 1 は 280～400 語前後、Book 2 では 320～470 語前後のまとまったパッセージを読みましょう。パッセージの長さは、Unit 1 から 12 にかけて少しずつ長くなるよう調整されています。初めて読む際には、時間を測りながら全体の内容を把握する練習をしてください。ページの下には、wpm（words per minute、1 分間当たりに読める単語数）を計算するための式が表示されています。毎ユニットの wpm の記録をとり、自分が内容を理解しながら読むことができる速さを把握しましょう。隣のページには、パッセージ中、太字で示されているキーワードの意味を確認する問題や、内容を確認する問題があります。内容確認問題は、基本的に 1 パラグラフにつき 1 題ずつ出題されています。読んだ内容を把握できているか確認しましょう。

❻ Writing Tips

　上記のパッセージのパラグラフ構成を理解するための穴埋め問題に回答し、英文ライティングのコツをつかみましょう。以下は、各ユニットで紹介されるライティングのコツです。

Unit	コツ	Unit	コツ
1	What is a paragraph?	7	Narrative essay
2	APA (1) Making a reference list	8	Persuasive essay
3	Formal vs. informal writing	9	APA (2) In-text citations
4	Different types of transitions	10	What is a good thesis statement?
5	Descriptive essay	11	Self-reflective writing
6	Written vs. spoken English	12	APA (3) When you paraphrase / don't paraphrase

❼ Writing Outline

　各ユニットに関連したトピックについて、自分の考えを書くためのアウトラインをまとめましょう。アウトラインは、基本的に「Introduction（導入）」と「Conclusion（結論）」の間に「Body（本論）」を挟み込む構成になっています。Writing Tips で学んだライティングのコツも参考にしながら、書きたい内容の枠組みを決めましょう。

CONTENTS

EnglishCentralのご案内

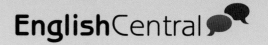

　本テキスト各ユニットの「Academic Reading」で学習する音声は、オンライン学習システム「EnglishCentral」で学習することができます。

　EnglishCentralでは動画の視聴や単語のディクテーションのほか、動画のセリフを音読し録音すると、コンピュータが発音を判定します。PCのwebだけでなく、スマートフォン、タブレットではアプリでも学習できます。リスニング、スピーキング、語彙力向上のため、ぜひ活用してください。

　EnglishCentralの利用にはアカウントとアクセスコードの登録が必要です。登録方法については下記ページにアクセスしてください。

（画像はすべてサンプルで、実際の教材とは異なります）

https://www.seibido.co.jp/englishcentral/pdf/ectextregister.pdf

見る

本文内でわからなかった単語は1クリックでその場で意味を確認

スロー再生

日英字幕（ON/OFF可）

学ぶ

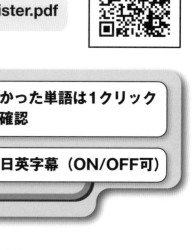

音声を聴いて空欄の単語をタイピング。ゲーム感覚で楽しく単語を覚える

話す

動画のセリフを音読し録音、コンピュータが発音を判定。

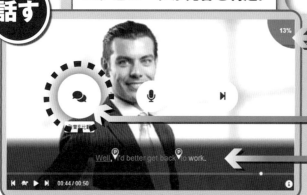

日本人向けに専門開発された音声認識によってスピーキング力を%で判定

ネイティブと自分が録音した発音を聞き比べ練習に生かすことができます

苦手な発音記号を的確に判断し、単語を緑、黄、赤の3色で表示

College Life

大学生活の意義について考えよう

Warm-up: *Share your ideas.*

What is the biggest challenge for you in college?

a. Managing time effectively.

b. Maintaining good grades.

c. Making new friends.

d. Choosing a career.

I chose answer _____ , because ....

....

....

....

Words in Focus: *Search the internet for words and phrases.* 1-02

❏ admission

❏ assignment

❏ bachelor's program

❏ department

❏ the OECD

❏ part-time job

❏ schedule

❏ sophomore

❏ student union

❏ survey

How do you manage your time?

 1-03

Welcome message from the union

STUDENT UNION

Jessie Miller (sophomore)

Welcome to our department! I'm Jessie, a second-year student. Time management is essential for students. How do you manage your time? Here are some tips for you about your weekly schedule, daily routine, and priorities.

Tip 1: SCHEDULE YOUR WEEK

You should try to get a clear image of your weekly schedule. Like most of you, I have a part-time job. But I work only on Sundays because I want to save weekdays for other things. For example, I ⬚ 1 ⬚ Monday evenings with the members of the Japanese-speaking club.

Tip 2: CREATE A ROUTINE

Keep regular sleep hours and get your life in rhythm. I get up at 7:00 every morning although I have no morning classes on Tuesdays and Fridays. So, I am ⬚ 2 ⬚ late for any classes. I also make it a rule to do yoga stretches before going to bed.

Tip 3: SET PRIORITIES

For us, studying should be the priority, right? I usually study in the library. But when I have no time during the day, I work at home to make sure I complete my assignments. When I have some spare time, I enjoy talking with my friends, watching movies, or playing video games.

This is how I manage my ⬚ 3 ⬚. Remember, effective time management plays a huge role in enriching your college life!

---

1. **Choose the best answer to complete the missing words in the passage.**

1. (A) spend	**2.** (A) always	**3.** (A) club
(B) spending	(B) never	(B) time
(C) to spend	(C) often	(C) sleep
(D) had spent	(D) sometimes	(D) friend

2. Read the passage and choose the best answer to each question.

1. Which of the following does Jessie NOT mention?
   (A) Which season to start the school year.
   (B) What to do on which day of the week.
   (C) What to do at which time of the day.
   (D) What is especially important.

2. Which activity does Jessie avoid doing on weekdays?
   (A) Working part-time.
   (B) Joining club activities.
   (C) Cooking for herself.
   (D) Doing yoga stretches.

3. Look at Jessie's schedule. What day is it?
   (A) Sunday.
   (B) Monday.
   (C) Tuesday.
   (D) Friday.

Reading Tips: *Main idea and details (1)*

読者にとって読みやすい英文の多くは、1つの段落（paragraph）内で議論する内容がはっきりと topic sentence として示され、それを説明するための詳細が述べられています。前ページの5つの段落それぞれの topic sentence を以下に書き出しましょう。

Paragraph	Topic sentence
1	Here are s_____ t_____ for you about your w_____ s_____, d_____ r_____, and p_____.
2	You should try to get a clear image of your w_____ s_____.
3	Keep regular sleep hours and g_____ y_____ l_____ in r_____.
4	For us, s_____ should be the p_____, right?
5	Remember, e_____ t_____ m_____ plays a huge role in e_____ y_____ c_____ l_____!

How old were you when you entered college?

Average age of new entrants to higher education

In Japan, most students **enroll** in bachelor's programs by the age of 20. However, this trend may be a rare case compared to the rest of the world. An international organization
5 (Organization for Economic Co-operation and Development, OECD) conducted a survey on the average age of first-time entrants to **tertiary education** in 43 countries. The chart shows some of the results from the 2017 survey. In Japan, the
10 average age of new students entering college is 18. This is the youngest among all the surveyed countries. This result can be explained by two reasons.

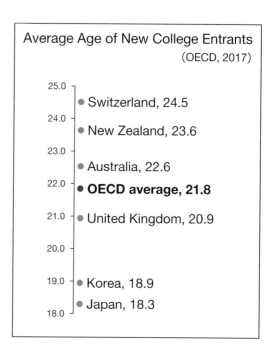

15 First, the OECD claims that it may be related to the Japanese life structure of three traditional stages: education, work, and **retirement**. Many Japanese students go straight to college from high school. Right after graduating from college, they often get a job. Many of them work in the same company for their entire life. Because of this tradition of a three-stage life, the average age of college students in Japan is kept very low.

20

Secondly, the OECD **mentions** the well-developed college admission system in Japan. Many different types of exams are offered as a way to enter universities. Some of them are quite flexible. Importantly, high school students are given opportunities to try different exams. Thanks to such a flexible system, it is relatively easy for Japanese high school students to go
25 on to college immediately after graduation.

In summary, the OECD's 2017 survey shows the **tendency** of Japanese students to enter college at a relatively early age. This low average age of entry can be explained by factors including the traditional way of life and the entrance examination system in Japan.

Your Reading Speed: **284** words ÷ _____ seconds × 60 = _____ wpm

Reference
OECD (2019). *Education at a glance 2019: OECD indicators*. OECD publishing, Paris. https://doi.org/10.1787/19991487

1. Choose the phrase that is related to each word / phrase.

1. enroll   (   )
2. tertiary education   (   )
3. retirement   (   )
4. mention   (   )
5. tendency   (   )

(a) a pattern
(b) the stage of life after finishing work
(c) to refer to something
(d) to register
(e) university and technical colleges

2. Read the passage and choose the best answer to each question.

1. Which of the following is mentioned about higher education in Japan?
    (A) All young people go to college.
    (B) Most first-year students are teenagers.
    (C) Students rarely go to college.
    (D) Many students are from foreign countries.

2. What did the OECD do?
    (A) They conducted an entrance exam for a university.
    (B) They carried out research in 43 countries.
    (C) They offered workplaces for young students.
    (D) They made programs for tertiary education.

3. What is the first explanation given by the OECD about Japanese students?
    (A) They start working after graduating from high school.
    (B) They often work part-time while in college.
    (C) They continue studying for their entire lives.
    (D) They tend to follow a similar life-stage pattern.

4. How does the OECD view Japan's admission system?
    (A) It needs to be developed further.
    (B) There are too many subjects to study.
    (C) It gives test takers a lot of possibilities.
    (D) It encourages students to drop out after entering school.

5. Which of the following is described in the passage?
    (A) The working style of OECD staff.
    (B) The age of college freshmen.
    (C) Education systems around the world.
    (D) How to enter and live in Japan.

Writing Tips: *What is a paragraph?*

英語で書くパラグラフ構成は「ハンバーガー」に例える事ができます。例えば、パラグラフ最初の topic sentence と最後の closing sentence はハンバーガーの上下のパンで、その間に detail 1 〜 3 という「具」が入っています。4 ページ第 3 パラグラフの構成をまとめてみましょう。

Topic sentence (パラグラフで説明する事の要約)	Secondly, the O_____ m_____ the w____-d_____ c____ a_____ s_____ in Japan.
Detail 1 (ポイント 1)	Many d_____ t_____ of e_____ are o_____ as a way to e_____ u_____.
Detail 2 (ポイント 2)	Some of them are q_____ f_____.
Detail 3 (ポイント 3)	Importantly, high school students are g_____ o_____ to t_____ d_____ e_____.
Closing sentence (説明したことの要約。Topic sentence と似た内容になる)	Thanks to such a flexible system, it is r_____ e_____ for J_____ h____ s____ s_____ to go on to college i_____ a____ g_____.

Writing Outline: *Main idea and details (1)*

CD 1-05

What is one thing that you would like to achieve in college? Explain the main idea, and add three details. Include a summary at the end.

Introduction	The one thing that I want to achieve in college is.... I will explain my goal, why I want to do this, and how I will achieve it.
Detail 1: [What]	To explain more clearly about my goal,....
Detail 2: [Why]	The reason that I want to do this is....
Detail 3: [How]	My plan to achieve this goal is....
Summary	By [time], I would like to [what], because [why]. I will [how].

UNIT 2

Understanding Copyright

著作権について考えよう

Warm-up: *Share your ideas.*

Which of the following do you consider to be the worst?

a. Copying a classmate's writing.

b. Copying entire articles from the internet.

c. Arriving late for class every week.

d. Sleeping while the teacher is talking.

I chose answer _____ , because ....

....

....

....

Words in Focus: *Search the internet for words and phrases.* 1-06

❏ cite

❏ consequences

❏ credit

❏ essay

❏ malfunction

❏ originality

❏ paper

❏ plagiarism

❏ struggle

❏ submit

Instructions for submitting written assignments.

Here are the instructions for turning in your first paper. Do not forget to have your paper checked for plagiarism. Make sure you do this [1] June 2nd, at 5 p.m.

1. Please go to the website, www.plagiarismchecker12.org
2. Log in using your student ID and password.
3. Click "Assignments," then go to "Dr. Montgomery's English Class."
4. Once you enter the class, you should see a button which says "Turn in [2]." Click it.
5. After you turn in the assignment, click "Immediately generate originality report" (NOT "Generate originality report after due date"). After this, click "Submit." This may take a while to process.
6. After steps 1–5, you should get your own originality report. This shows you what percentage of your paper is written in your own words. Make sure your originality percentage is well above 70%. If not, try to rewrite direct quotes with your own words. Then, repeat steps 4–5.

If you have any questions about the use of the website, contact me at montgomery@gdail.org well before the [3]. You should not do the task just before it is due. Your Wi-Fi or your computer could malfunction, or the webpage could be busy. None of these incidents can be an excuse for late papers.

1. **Choose the best answer to complete the missing words in the passage.**

1. (A) no earlier than
   (B) no later than
   (C) no less than
   (D) no more than

2. (A) assignment
   (B) button
   (C) class
   (D) password

3. (A) dead end
   (B) dead zone
   (C) deadline
   (D) deadlock

2. Read the passage and choose the best answer to each question.

1. What do you do if the originality report is below 70%?
   (A) Log in.
   (B) Click "Submit."
   (C) Revise the paper.
   (D) Start on a new paper.

2. Which is NOT a possible problem with submitting a paper?
   (A) Connection to the internet.
   (B) Access to the web page.
   (C) Operation of a device.
   (D) A warning from the teacher.

3. Look at the plagiarism report. What can be inferred from these results?
   (A) This paper is 78% correct.
   (B) 22% of this paper is original.
   (C) The paper received a B.
   (D) There are three online references.

> Plagiarism Checker
>
> Originality report
> **78%**
>
> Identical matches:
> ✓ https://en.vikipe
> ✓ https://books.g
> ✓ https://scholar.g

Reading Tips: *Dealing with unknown words*

英文を読んでいて知らない単語に出くわした時、前後の文から意味を推測しながら読み進めていく習慣をつけると、英語を英語で考え、素早く読み進めることにつながります。前ページで示されている "originality report" に関する文を書き出し、これが何なのか推測してみましょう。

Originality report とは？（文脈）	（推測）
A_____ you turn in the a_____, click…	課題提出後に行うもの。
"I_____ generate originality report" NOT "Generate originality report a_____ d_____ d_____"	提出直後／期限後という２種類の方法がある。
This shows you w_____ p_____ of your p_____ is w_____ in y_____ o_____ w_____.	自分の言葉で書いた単語の比率が示される。
Make sure your originality percentage is w_____ a_____ _____%.	70% を超えるべき。
If n_____, t_____ to r_____ direct quotes w_____ y_____ o_____ w_____.	超えていなければ書き直す必要がある。

Plagiarism and its consequences

Plagiarism is when you use somebody's work as your own, without giving them credit for it. For college students, it often happens in their homework assignments. Some students think this is an easy way to hand in homework, and others try to do it after they **struggle** with an assignment. In this essay, we will go over how plagiarism in writing is **detected**, and also the
5   consequences that come with it.

First, how is plagiarism **detected**? Sometimes, it can be found by teachers because the writing is "too good." Teachers know their students' English proficiency, so submitting an essay that is too well written is proof that the student didn't write it. If students copy each
10   other's essays, teachers can usually tell, because they look very similar.

Another way teachers can find plagiarism is by using detection websites. When teachers copy and paste the student's essay onto the website, it gives them a percentage of how much of the essay is **plagiarized**. The detection website scans various books, websites, and other
15   students' essays to do this.

Now, we will discuss the consequences of plagiarism. First, the **plagiarized** writing assignment will receive a score of zero, with no re-submission. Second, some schools will expel or suspend students. Others will give a failing grade for that class. In the end, though, the
20   biggest **punishment** might be that the student will lose their trustworthiness. That is, teachers may never believe what the student says.

In conclusion, plagiarism is the act of stealing someone's work without giving them credit. There can be many different consequences for plagiarizing, and ultimately it leads to
25   the student losing trust from others. To avoid this, students need to correctly **cite** information, and to ask for help on an assignment.

Your Reading Speed: **295** words ÷ _____ seconds × 60 = _____ wpm

1. Choose the phrase that is related to each word / phrase.

1. struggle   (   )
2. detect   (   )
3. plagiarize   (   )
4. punishment   (   )
5. cite   (   )

(a) consequence for bad behavior
(b) to pretend that someone else's work is your own
(c) to experience difficulty
(d) to find or discover
(e) to give credit to an author or creator

2. Read the passage and choose the best answer to each question.

1. What is plagiarism?
   (A) Copying from others without permission.
   (B) Writing many research papers.
   (C) Handing in homework quickly.
   (D) Struggling to write.

2. How can a teacher detect plagiarism in a student essay?
   (A) It is very long.
   (B) It is very short.
   (C) It has citations.
   (D) Its quality is too high.

3. What do detection websites do?
   (A) Show which website to use.
   (B) Copy and paste your essay.
   (C) Finish your homework.
   (D) Find copying in your essay.

4. According to the passage, what is the worst consequence of plagiarism?
   (A) You will get a zero score for the assignment.
   (B) You will fail the class.
   (C) Your teacher will be angry.
   (D) Nobody will trust you anymore.

5. What is the author's suggestion for dealing with writing assignments?
   (A) Use modern technology.
   (B) Trust your friends.
   (C) Cite information correctly.
   (D) Have your friends use your work.

Writing Tips: *APA (1) Making a reference list*

レポートが plagiarism (剽窃) と見なされないためには、レポートの最後に reference list (参考文献リスト) を掲載し、参考にした文献を全て示すことが必要です。以下の参考文献について、著者の姓、出版年、文献のタイトルを書き出しましょう。

著者の姓	出版年	文献タイトル
＿＿＿＿＿		＿＿＿ ＿＿＿＿＿ ＿＿＿＿＿.
＿＿＿＿, ＿＿＿＿, & ＿＿＿＿＿		＿＿＿＿＿-＿＿ ＿＿＿＿.
＿＿＿＿＿		＿＿＿ ＿＿＿＿ ＿＿＿＿ ＿＿＿: Plagiarism by university students—literature and lessons.

References

Howard, R. M. (1992). A plagiarism pentimento. *Journal of Teaching Writing*, *11*(2), 233-45.

Maurer, H. A., Kappe, F., & Zaka, B. (2006). Plagiarism—A survey. *Journal of Universal Computer Science*, *12*(8), 1050-1084.

Park, C. (2003). In other (people's) words: Plagiarism by university students—literature and lessons. *Assessment & Evaluation in Higher Education*, *28*(5), 471-488.

Writing Outline: *Giving reasons* 1-09

What would you say if your friends suggested you copy each other's assignment? Why is it wrong to do so? Give two reasons. Add at least one reference to support your ideas.

Introduction	If my friends suggested we copy each other's homework, I would decline by saying.... There are two reasons for this. First, [**reason 1**]. Second, [**reason 2**].
Reason 1	Copying somebody's assignment is... because [**reason 1**].
Reason 2	Next, finishing your assignment is important because [**reason 2**].
Conclusion	In my opinion,....
References	

Cyberbullying

ネットいじめについて考えよう

Warm-up: *Share your ideas.*

What do you think should be the punishment for cyberbullying?

a. Bullies should be fined.

b. Bullies should be sentenced to prison.

c. Bullies should be expelled from school.

d. Bullies should not be punished.

I chose answer _____ , because ....
....
....
....

Words in Focus: *Search the internet for words and phrases.* 1-10

- ❏ ban
- ❏ benefit
- ❏ blackmail
- ❏ cell phone
- ❏ chat

- ❏ cheat
- ❏ cyberbullying
- ❏ foul
- ❏ monitor
- ❏ stalking

What counts as cyberbullying?

 1-11

Subject	**RE: Ken, are you OK?**
Date	26/06/2024 23:48
To	Lily
Attachment(s)	20240618_2135.jpg

Dear Lily,

Thanks for caring about me! I'll tell you what happened between Greg and me at our part-time job. Last Tuesday night, he tried to blackmail me into changing ___1___ with him. Please see the attached file. It's a chat conversation between us.

Do you think he's bullying me? I've never ___2___ on any exam, and I don't think I did anything that was suspicious. His "proof" worries me a little though.

I really don't know what to do next. If I listen to Greg, I think he's going to make me his servant for the rest of my college life. Maybe our job manager could help, but that might upset Greg even more. I don't want college professors to know because it might damage my reputation.

___3___ of all, I'll have to see him in class tomorrow. What do you think I should do?

Ken

---

1. Choose the best answer to complete the missing words in the passage.

1. (A) hands	**2.** (A) cheated	**3.** (A) Best
(B) minds	(B) passed	(B) First
(C) names	(C) studied	(C) Least
(D) shifts	(D) worked	(D) Worst

2. Read the passage and choose the best answer to each question.

1. In the email, what is Ken asking Lily to do?
   (A) To damage the professor's reputation.
   (B) To help Greg with his exam.
   (C) To stop bullying Greg.
   (D) To give him advice.

2. Why does Ken say, "That doesn't make any sense"?
   (A) He doesn't know what the exam will be about.
   (B) He doesn't understand why he should take the shift.
   (C) He has proof that he cheated.
   (D) He has a good sense of humor.

3. Look at the chat message on the right. What happened?
   (A) Ken sent a message to Greg.
   (B) Lily sent a message to Ken.
   (C) Greg started a rumor about Ken.
   (D) The manager started a rumor about Ken.

Ken

G Hey, you know this guy? He cheated on his last exam.
G
N What?! We've gotta punish him.
T I knew you were gonna do that, Ken!
W Get lost, K.
E Nobody's gonna be on your side.

Reading Tips: *Cause and effect*

英文を読むにあたっては、文中の cause and effect（原因と結果）を頭の中でイメージすることにより、内容理解がより早く進みます。例えば前ページに掲載されているメールの件名は "RE:" で始まっていることから、最初にリリーが "Ken, are you OK?" というメールを送信した結果、ケンが返信をしていることがイメージできます。メール本文の中では、ケンが心配していることを 3 つ挙げています。どのような原因がどのような結果を招くことを心配しているのか、書き出してみましょう。

Cause (原因)	Effect (ケンが心配している結果)
If I l_____ to G_____,	I think he's going to m_____ m____ h___ s_____ for the rest of my college life.
Maybe our j____ m_____ c_____ h_____,	but that might u_____ G_____ e_____ m_____.
I don't want c_____ p_____ to k_____	because it might d_____ my r_____.

Smartphones and cyberbullying

Should smartphones be banned from schools? There are **benefits** of owning smartphones, because parents always want a way to contact their children in an emergency. However, smartphone use can lead to bullying. This includes **foul** language, stalking, threatening people, and putting others' embarrassing actions on the web. This essay will
5   describe how people argue for and against banning smartphones from schools.

First, one argument for banning smartphones is that banning works better than other means of control. In New York City, for example, public schools tried a "Misuse It, You Lose It" policy. With this policy, students were allowed to use their cell phones, but lost this
10   **privilege** if they didn't use them correctly. However, there were fewer cases of cyberbullying when cell phones were banned, compared to when this policy was put in place (Riley, 2017). This could suggest that a ban itself works better than any other kind of policy.

Second, others are against the idea that we should ban smartphones from schools.
15   Their argument is that a smartphone can be a good educational tool, especially when students cannot **afford** to buy computers (Drabwell, 2018). Teachers can easily give students handouts and write feedback on their assignments with the help of smartphone applications.

In addition, smartphones are useful tools from a student's point of view. They can
20   hand in assignments with their phones, and also do some quick research on the web when they need to write a paper. It seems such a waste not to use this tool, when so many students own one already.

In conclusion, there are very good arguments for and against the **claim** that we should
25   ban smartphones from schools. Schools need to decide if they want to monitor students' smartphone use so they can responsibly use them, or shield their students from these devices.

Your Reading Speed: **305** words ÷ _____ seconds × 60 = _____ wpm

References
Drabwell, C. (2018, July 25). *6 tips for teachers on using mobile phones in classrooms*. The Open University.
Riley, N. S. (2017, February 6). *To fight cyberbullying, ban cellphones from school*. New York Post.

1. **Choose the phrase that is related to each word / phrase.**

1. benefit	( )		**(a)** a positive outcome
2. foul	( )		**(b)** an advantage
3. privilege	( )		**(c)** rude, disgusting
4. afford	( )		**(d)** to have enough money for
5. claim	( )		**(e)** to state that something is true

2. **Read the passage and choose the best answer to each question.**

1. What is one advantage of having smartphones?
   (A) Students in different countries are using them.
   (B) Parents can contact their children.
   (C) Recent models have fast Wi-Fi.
   (D) Their use can lead to bullying.

2. What is true about banning smartphones?
   (A) It worked better than other policies.
   (B) It helped students not to lose their smartphones.
   (C) It granted privileges to smartphone users.
   (D) It resulted in an increase in cases of bullying.

3. Who is most likely to be against the idea of banning smartphones from school?
   (A) Teachers in New York.
   (B) Riley.
   (C) Drabwell.
   (D) The author of this essay.

4. Why does the author say "It seems such a waste"?
   (A) Because students often break their smartphones.
   (B) Because smartphones are too expensive.
   (C) Because most students own this useful tool.
   (D) Because most students have bad eyesight.

5. What does the author suggest at the end about smartphones?
   (A) They should be banned.
   (B) Schools should decide their own policy.
   (C) They should be used educationally.
   (D) You shouldn't buy them.

Writing Tips: *Formal vs. informal writing*

レポートや論文を書く時には、短縮形や会話調の表現を避けるなど、英文ライティングの形式を守ってフォーマルな書き方をすると、説得力が増します。以下は、16 ページの第 2, 3, 4 段落のトピックセンテンスをインフォーマルな形式に書き換えたものです。元の文章から下線部の語を書き出し、違いを確認しましょう。

Paragraph	Formal	Informal な言い換え
2	First, o_____ a_____ for b_____ s_____ is that b_____ w____ b_____ than o____ m_____ of c_____.	Some people say, "Don't let your kids use smartphones," 'cause they think that's the best way.
3	Second, o_____ a____ a_____ the i_____ that we should ban smartphones from schools.	But others say, "Why not?!" They don't wanna ban smartphones from school.
4	I____ a_____, smartphones are useful tools f_____ _____ s_____ p_____ o____ v_____.	Also, if I were a student, I would think smartphones are useful.

Writing Outline: *Cause and effect*

Write an email to an elderly family member or friend about cyberbullying. What is one cause? What is one effect? What is one way to avoid cyberbullying?

Introduction	Dear [name / relation], have you ever heard of cyberbullying? It's really troubling my generation.
Cause	One of the causes of this problem is....
Effect	Cyberbullying is a problem because....
Avoidance strategy	What we can do to avoid this problem is....
Final message	So, cyberbullying is a problem because [**effect**]. However, [**avoidance strategy**]....

Tourism

快適な旅のコツについて考えよう

Warm-up: *Share your ideas.*

What worries you most about visiting a new country?

a. Using a different system of money.

b. Eating unfamiliar food.

c. Riding public transportation.

d. Upsetting local people.

I chose answer _____ , because ....
....
....
....

Words in Focus: *Search the internet for words and phrases.*

 1-14

❏ cash

❏ gallon

❏ the hospitality industry

❏ measurement

❏ mile

❏ pound

❏ regular customer

❏ temperature

❏ tipping system

❏ wage

Metric and imperial measurements

So you're going to the States? If you're driving, you'll need gallons of gas to travel hundreds of miles on the highway. Temperatures  can go over 100 degrees Fahrenheit in the summer. So, grab a cold drink with a quarter-pounder burger at the gas station. Are you following so far? Are there any words you can't understand easily?

If you are [**1**] kilograms, meters, and liters, you are using the metric system. Things are measured in units of ten. On the other hand, measurements such as ounces, yards, and fluid ounces are used in the [**2**] system. There are three countries in the world using only imperial measurement systems now: Liberia, Myanmar, and the USA.

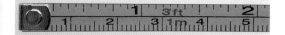

In the 1790s, the metric system was introduced in France in order to make life easier. It soon spread to most of the world. The UK also adopted the system in 1965, but many people there still prefer imperial measurements. So, you'll have to order beer by the pint in a British pub. Driving along the motorway, distances are measured in miles. If you stay there long enough, you might become good at using both systems!

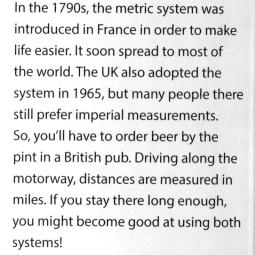

Are you going somewhere which has a different measurement system? Why not download a conversion app on your phone? Happy traveling—and don't forget to [**3**] those air miles!

1. **Choose the best answer to complete the missing words in the passage.**

1. (A) use to
   (B) use up
   (C) used up
   (D) used to

2. (A) accurate
   (B) imperial
   (C) metric
   (D) temperature

3. (A) add
   (B) do
   (C) save
   (D) select

2. Read the passage and choose the best answer to each question.

1. Which of the following is NOT true about the USA?
   (A) Summer can be hot.
   (B) The imperial system is used now.
   (C) The metric system is used there.
   (D) Distance is measured in miles.

2. Which of the following statements gives evidence that the metric system "makes life easier"?
   (A) Kilograms are counted in units of ten.
   (B) The imperial system is from the UK.
   (C) Distances are measured in miles.
   (D) You might learn both systems.

3. Which function of the app shown in the illustration would NOT be used to convert measurements described in the text?
   (A) Volume.　　(B) Temperature.　　(C) Time.　　(D) Weight.

Reading Tips: *Understanding timelines*

文章の内容を素早く把握するために、そこに書かれている時系列の情報（timeline）を整理する手法があります。前ページの文章から timeline を示すヒントを書き出し、現在の話なのか過去の話なのか、時制を整理しましょう。

段落	Hints	現在？過去？
1	If you're d_____, you'll n____ gallons of gas to travel hundreds of miles on the highway.	
2	Things a____ m_____ in units of ten.	
3	In the 1_____, the metric system w____ i_____ in France in order to make life easier.	
3	It s____ s_____ to most of the world.	
3	The UK also a_____ the system in 1_____,	
3	but many people there s_____ p_____ imperial measurements.	
3	So, you'll h_____ t____ o_____ beer by the pint in a British pub.	
4	A____ y____ g_____ somewhere which has a different measurement system?	

Why do we tip?

In Japan, around 70% of university students have part-time jobs. This compares to 81% in the US. In other words, the **majority** of students are working part-time in both countries. However, when working in the service industry, there is a difference between Japan and the United States in the wages that students can earn. Students in Japan are generally paid an

5   hourly wage, while students in the US also rely on tips. Although it can be confusing at first, tipping provides benefits for both the staff and customers.

Research shows that wait staff make very little money in the US. Some restaurants allow their staff to take home all of their tips. In this case, hardworking servers make the most

10   money. Other stores share all tips equally with each staff member who worked on a **particular** shift.

Whichever system is used, the employer gains the largest percentage of money earned. In the hospitality **industry**, these employers pay many staff very little, using tip money to top

15   up wages. That is one reason to always tip when you eat out.

In addition, popular bars on weekend evenings are crowded with people waiting to order drinks. One effective way of getting served is to wave a rolled-up cash bill. Likewise, in a restaurant with table service, regular customers who are known to tip well get good service. In

20   the worst case, some staff will be quite **rude** to non-tipping diners. You can show how satisfied you are by the size of your tip.

Many aspects of the tipping system are unfamiliar to people who come from cultures like Japan. However, visitors to countries like the US need to understand that tipping **leads to**

25   fair conditions for people in employment, and better service for customers. When eating out, make sure you have enough money for tipping to help the low-paid workers who serve you, and help yourself at the same time.

Your Reading Speed: **322** words ÷ _____ seconds × 60 = _____ wpm

1. **Choose the phrase that is related to each word / phrase.**

1. majority   (   )
2. particular   (   )
3. industry   (   )
4. rude   (   )
5. lead to   (   )

(a) 50% or more
(b) bad-mannered
(c) specific
(d) to cause
(e) type of business

2. **Read the passage and choose the best answer to each question.**

1. What is one similarity between Japanese and American students?
   (A) They are well paid.
   (B) They work part-time.
   (C) They rely on basic wages.
   (D) They receive tips.

2. Which of the following is NOT a system for distributing tip money?
   (A) Workers keep all tips.
   (B) Employers keep it all.
   (C) Hard workers receive more money.
   (D) Tips are shared equally.

3. Who makes the most money from the tipping system?
   (A) Customers.
   (B) Hardworking servers.
   (C) Staff who don't work hard.
   (D) Employers.

4. What does the writer recommend as a good way to get served in a crowded bar?
   (A) Calling the bartender in a loud voice.
   (B) Putting some money in the tips jar.
   (C) Waiting for your turn.
   (D) Waving some money around.

5. What does the article give as the main reason for tipping?
   (A) To help owners.
   (B) There is no reason.
   (C) To help wait staff.
   (D) To visit foreign countries.

Writing Tips: *Different types of transitions*

Transition (転換語) を使うことにより、話の流れを分かりやすくすることができます。下の表を埋めながら、22 ページの文章の最初のパラグラフで使われている transition の役割を考えましょう。

Transition	Transition が使われている文を抜粋しましょう。
In other words (言い換えると)	I___ o_____ w_____, t__ m_____ o__ s_____ are working part-time in b_____ c_____.
However (しかし)	H_____, when working in the service industry, t_____ i____ d_____ b_____ J_____ a___ t___ U___ S_____ in the wages that students can earn.
while (〜に対して)	Students in Japan are g_____ p____ a____ h_____ w____, w____ students in the US a_____ r_____ o__ t____.
Although (けれども)	A_____ it can be c_____ a_ f_____, tipping p_____ b_____ f__ b__ t__ s_____ a____ c_____.

Writing Outline: *Following timelines* 1-17

Write a short history of a place for tourists you know well. Explain three different events or eras.

Introduction	You'll have a great time visiting [place]. Do you know anything about its history? Three important milestones were [**milestone 1**], [**milestone 2**], and [**milestone 3**].
Milestone 1	First, in [time]....
Milestone 2	Later, in [time]....
Milestone 3	Most recently, in [time]....
Summary	So when you visit [place], remember [**milestone 1**], [**milestone 2**], and [**milestone 3**]. If you are interested, you can....

Foreign Encounters

異文化体験について考えよう

Warm-up: *Share your ideas.*

How do you feel about the idea of studying abroad?

a. It's exciting.

b. I'd be nervous.

c. It sounds too hard for me.

d. I do not want to go abroad.

I chose answer _____ , because ....
....
....
....

Words in Focus: *Search the internet for words and phrases.* 1-18

❏ abroad

❏ adjustment

❏ cultural awareness

❏ culture shock

❏ dorm

❏ online application

❏ overseas

❏ resident

❏ room service

❏ satisfaction

UniDorm.com

Let us offer you a room of your choice.

One of the main ⬚1⬚ you'll have to make when studying abroad is where to stay. Living with a local family is reliable and safe. However, the size of the house, food standard, and location will vary. Staying in a hotel is usually clean and comfortable. But it can be lonely and you will need extra money for eating out or room service.

If you are looking for a safe, reasonable, and comfortable experience, look no further than UniDorms. You'll have a cozy bed with a desk. You'll also share a bathroom, kitchen and study areas with five other students. Housemates come from a variety of backgrounds. ⬚2⬚, you can learn about their culture and share information about your own. Residents often hold international cooking parties in their apartments.

Before applying for one of our ⬚3⬚ desirable UniDorms, please consider the following questions to complete our online application.

Step 1: Choose from Private (individual bedrooms) or Shared (two students share a bedroom). We work hard to match residents.

Step 2: Do you drive? You can apply for a UniDorm with or without a car park.

Step 3: What location are you looking for? We have 30 sites across New Zealand.

Step 4: When do you plan to stay? In our peak season of September/October, rooms can fill up from around four months in advance.

Step 5: Click on the "Go" button, and we will search our database to find the best plan for you.

1. **Choose the best answer to complete the missing words in the passage.**

1. (A) decide
(B) decided
(C) decision
(D) decisions

2. (A) Therefore
(B) However
(C) Then
(D) Because

3. (A) lot
(B) highly
(C) much
(D) far

2. Read the passage and choose the best answer to each question.

1. Which is given as a benefit of staying with a local family?
   (A) It is secure.
   (B) The house is big.
   (C) The food is good.
   (D) It is clean.

2. Which is NOT a reason to stay at a UniDorm?
   (A) The cost.
   (B) The cultural experience.
   (C) The private kitchen.
   (D) The options for location.

3. Look at the advertisement. Which room is it?
   (A) An individual bedroom.
   (B) A shared room.
   (C) A room without a car park.
   (D) A room not in their database.

Single bedroom
From **NZ$ 170** per week

 Private room
 Shared bathroom
 Wi-Fi
P Parking

On each floor:
· Shared bathrooms
· Shared kitchen facilities
· Dining and study areas

Reading Tips: *Similarities and differences*

文中に述べられている事象を similarities (類似点) と differences (相違点) で仕分けすると効率よく情報整理ができます。以下の表は、前ページで取り上げられている homestay, hotel, dormitory について述べられていることを整理したものです。文中で述べられていないことがらについて、あなたの考えで Yes / No どちらかを記入し、3 つの宿泊形態の similarities と differences をまとめましょう。

	Homestay	Hotel	Dormitory
Reliable?			
Safe?			
Clean?			
Comfortable?			
May feel lonely?			
Extra money for food?			
Shared bathroom?			

The U-curve and the W-curve

Participants in study abroad programs are able to develop their language abilities and cultural **awareness**. However, not all programs are totally positive. In fact, many students who go abroad to study experience a variety of emotions. These feelings tend to follow a certain kind of pattern, which is known as a U-curve.

5

The U-curve describes four **common** stages. The first stage is called the "honeymoon period." People are excited about their new lives overseas. Stage two is referred to as "culture shock." They struggle to understand the new culture and wish to return home. Stage three is known as "adjustment." People recognize the positive **aspects** of their new situation and make

10 changes to live more comfortably. The final stage, "mastery," refers to people who are living comfortably as members of their new community.

A diagram, showing the level of adjustment changing by time, makes a U-shape. It takes about two years in total. The first and last stages are at the top, and the period of culture

15 shock is at the bottom.

Later, the W-curve was described. This is an **extension** of the U-curve. It includes the experience of the person after returning home from living abroad. Life satisfaction continues after they get back home. However, "reverse culture shock" is a common problem. People

20 miss aspects of the culture that they experienced abroad and wish that their home country was more like it. Like the U-curve, this reverse culture shock is usually followed by a second period of adjustment. In this "re-adjustment" stage, the returnees finally feel satisfied with their home culture once again.

25 Students who leave their country to study overseas can prepare themselves by learning about the U- and W- curves. It is only a general pattern, but it is **comforting** to know that culture shock is normal and that satisfaction with life tends to increase after a while. In addition, it is important to understand that culture shock can occur in the home country, and this too will be replaced by more positive feelings. Therefore, talking about these feelings with

30 classmates is recommended as a way to adjust more smoothly.

Your Reading Speed: **358** words ÷ _____ seconds × 60 = _____ wpm

1. Choose the phrase that is related to each word / phrase.

1. awareness   (   )
2. common   (   )
3. aspect   (   )
4. extension   (   )
5. comforting   (   )

(a) a condition
(b) experienced by all
(c) making something longer
(d) reassuring
(e) understanding

2. Read the passage and choose the best answer to each question.

1. What is the U-curve?
   (A) A stage.
   (B) A pattern.
   (C) A study abroad program.
   (D) A piece of advice.

2. Which of the following is not true about the U-curve?
   (A) The first stage involves positive feelings.
   (B) The second stage involves feelings of unease.
   (C) The third stage is harder than the second stage.
   (D) The fourth stage is the last one.

3. What takes around two years?
   (A) The first and last stages.
   (B) The U-curve.
   (C) The W-curve.
   (D) The period of culture shock.

4. What is the main difference between the U-curve and the W-curve?
   (A) The U-curve applies only to returnees.
   (B) The W-curve has more stages than the U-curve.
   (C) The U-curve involves a "reverse culture shock" period.
   (D) The W-curve is shorter than the U-curve.

5. What does the author suggest?
   (A) Studying abroad.
   (B) Spending around two years in another country.
   (C) Positive thinking.
   (D) Talking to other students.

Writing Tips: *Descriptive essay*

Descriptive essay では状況をただ説明するのではなく、人や場所、物事や気持ちなどを五感を使って描写することがポイントです。下のチャートは 28 ページで説明されている U-curve の最初の 2 段階を描写したものです。下線部にふさわしい語を語群から選び、それぞれの段階がどのように描写されているか考えましょう。

Stages	Descriptive essay
1. h _____ p _____	When I went to study abroad, everything looked like a scene from a _____. There were huge _____ in the streets advertising Broadway _____; everybody walking was _____ different langages; the taxis _____ in the distance were a _____ color. It was such a cool _____. [honking movie musicals sight signs speaking yellow]
2. c _____ s _____	This didn't last very long, however. Culture shock _____ me when I _____ a convenience store. I _____ some soda to the cashier, but the guy didn't even _____ at me. I _____ him I wanted to buy it, and he grunted. Then, he _____ some change at me, with a _____ on his face. [brought frown look struck threw told visited]

Writing Outline: *Similarities and differences*

Write about the similarities and differences between two countries. If you like, one of these can be your own country.

Introduction	You may feel uncomfortable when you visit [Country A] because.... I would like to focus on the similarities and differences between [Country A] and [Country B].
Similarities	One thing that [Country A] and [Country B] have in common is [similarity]....
Differences	On the other hand, they have differences in.... For example, [difference]....
Conclusion	To overcome this uneasiness,....

Entertainment

娯楽について考えよう

Warm-up: *Share your ideas.*

What is important for you when deciding whether or not to watch a movie?

   a. The actors and directors.
   b. The soundtrack.
   c. The movie trailer.
   d. Reviews of the movie.

I chose answer _____ , because ....
....
....
....

Words in Focus: *Search the internet for words and phrases.*   1-22

❏ animated   ❏ cruel
❏ aquarium   ❏ *Dumbo* (the movie)
❏ audience   ❏ soundtrack
❏ big top   ❏ star
❏ circus   ❏ theme

Best fantasy adventure ever! ★★★★★

This will be a hit with viewers of all ages. Stevens and Edwards star as drummers in the high school band. One day, while they are practicing, a mysterious creature comes out of their drums. He invites them inside. The musicians go on a trip through a world of guitar-playing monkeys, singing snakes and orchestra-conducting bats. The action is non-stop. The heroes learn ⬚ 1 ⬚ lessons about music from animated beasts. The script is laugh-out-loud funny. The soundtrack is so beautiful that it made me cry! The ending will shock and surprise as the unexpected takes place. Children learning to play musical instruments will love the young heroes. They might even wish that they too could step inside a magic drum.

THE MAGIC DRUM

STARRING
**Tom Stevens
Peter Edwards**

DIRECTOR
**Claudia
Spielstone**

Released March 23

Certificate U :
Any age group from 4 years.
Contains mild violence and language.

Better avoid this one. ★☆☆☆☆

Spielstone hasn't made a movie in five years. Her fans have been ⬚ 2 ⬚ for this! Her previous releases were quite enjoyable. They were cheery films for young audiences. This one is not. Uh… it's rather disappointing and unoriginal. The ugly bat who comes out of their drums is incredibly irritating. Moreover, the animators were completely lacking in imagination. There is nothing remarkable to look at. The animals who our "heroes" meet are one-dimensional. There is no character development at all! The composer had an opportunity to use the musical themes of the story to create a kid-friendly, sing-along soundtrack. Unfortunately, all of the music is instrumental. Like the film, it is unlikely to have any ⬚ 3 ⬚.

1. Choose the best answer to complete the missing words in the passage.

1. (A) disappointing
(B) disproving
(C) fascinating
(D) frightening

2. (A) waiting
(B) waited
(C) watching
(D) watched

3. (A) failure
(B) movie
(C) music
(D) success

2. Read the passage and choose the best answer to each question.

1. What do the two reviews suggest about the movie?

   (A) It features endangered species from around the world.

   (B) It was the first film Claudia Spielstone made.

   (C) Children are not allowed to watch this movie.

   (D) It received both positive and negative reviews.

2. Why did the second reviewer come to the conclusion "avoid this one?"

   (A) Because the characters are not interesting.

   (B) Because the tickets are too expensive.

   (C) Because audiences had to wait five years.

   (D) Because the music is unoriginal.

3. Look at the soundtrack album artwork. Which one of the reviews may contain untrue information?

   (A) "Best fantasy adventure ever."

   (B) "Better avoid this one."

   (C) Both (A) and (B).

   (D) Neither of the above.

Reading Tips: *Categorizing*

文章から情報を抜き出してまとめる際に、categorizing という手法が役に立ちます。前ページの 2 つのレビューを見直し、以下の 4 つの特徴に関する内容をまとめましょう。

Feature	First reviewer	Second reviewer
Overall rating	This will be a h____ with v_____ of a___ a____.	Uh… it's rather d_____ and u_____.
The bat	One day, while they are practicing, a m_____ c_____ comes out of their drums.	The u_____ b____ who comes out of their drums is i_____ i_____.
Three animals	The musicians go on a trip through a world of g_____-p_____ m_____, s_____ s_____ and o_____-c_____ b_____.	The animals who our "heroes" meet are o____-d_____. There is n___ c_____ d_____ at all!
The soundtrack	The soundtrack is s_____ b_____.	U_____, all of the music is i_____.

Circus – fun for all?

Movies such as *the Greatest Showman* (2017) and *Dumbo* (1941, 2019) show families going to visit a "big top" tent. Inside, they are entertained by human and animal performers. However, there is growing evidence of the **cruelty** suffered by circus animals. The traditional circus does not provide ethical entertainment. On the other hand, recent changes have led to
5   a reduction in harm to unwilling animals. It is hoped that governments around the world will soon bring this cruel practice to an end.

In the story of *Dumbo*, many of the senior elephants in the circus are comfortable and satisfied with their lives. This is different from reality. In 1916, an elephant called Mary was
10   killed in public in Tennessee, USA. She had attacked a circus worker. Eighty years later, another elephant, Tyke, was shot dead on the streets of Honolulu. This was because he had escaped from a circus. Even so, elephants continue to appear in circuses in many countries. Circus workers **beat** them with sticks in order to make them do tricks. The animals are forced to suffer in uncomfortable conditions. Tigers, lions, camels, and other animals are also
15   mistreated.

Despite the problems associated with circuses, they remain a source of entertainment. However, more **modern** circuses show different **attitudes** toward their performers. Only human cast members work for the circus, and they receive training and a salary. They can retire from
20   the circus when they choose.

Moreover, show producers have developed a large number of different events, with themes such as the Beatles, Christmas, or an action thriller. While animal-based circuses continue to feature the same tired, cruel performances, the **modern** circus actually offers much
25   more variety through its all-human cast.

In many urban places there is little chance to see animals as beautiful and unique as elephants or tigers. Hollywood movies add to this desire, by showing the circus as a place of wonder. However, circuses, like zoos and aquariums, have been shown to be places where
30   animals suffer for human entertainment. This **ancient** form of entertainment is no longer acceptable. The practice of animals performing in circuses must be stopped soon.

> Your Reading Speed: **359** words ÷ _____ seconds × 60 = _____ wpm

1. **Choose the phrase that is related to each word / phrase.**

1. cruelty   (   )   **(a)** ill-treatment

2. beat   (   )   **(b)** to hit repeatedly

3. modern   (   )   **(c)** recent, new

4. attitude   (   )   **(d)** very old

5. ancient   (   )   **(e)** way of looking at things

2. **Read the passage and choose the best answer to each question.**

1. What is discussed in this essay?

(A) How to enjoy movies.

(B) How to become a top performer.

(C) Ethical entertainment.

(D) Governments around the world.

2. Which of the following describes the movie *Dumbo*?

(A) There are many performers.

(B) One elephant kills a human.

(C) The animals all look happy.

(D) Older elephants are comfortable.

3. What is true about modern circuses?

(A) There are no problems anymore.

(B) Human cast members are unpaid.

(C) Performers may quit at any time.

(D) Attitudes are the same as in the past.

4. Which statement applies to modern circuses?

(A) Animals are always involved.

(B) They are shown in movie theaters.

(C) They have different themes.

(D) Audiences perform various tricks.

5. What is the main conclusion of this essay?

(A) People love to see elephants and tigers.

(B) A circus is a wonderful place.

(C) There are few animals in large cities.

(D) We must not harm animals for entertainment.

Writing Tips: *Written vs. spoken English*

英語の書き言葉は、話し言葉とは異なります。話し言葉では短い文を接続詞などでつなぎながら並べ、途中に言いよどみや繰り返しが起こることがありますが、書き言葉では、語句や文法、文全体の構造を工夫して、論理的に伝える必要があります。以下は、34ページの文章の第2, 3, 4段落のトピックセンテンスを話し言葉に言い換えたものです。下線部の語を埋め、違いをまとめましょう。

Written (Circus- fun for all?)	Spoken (言い換え)
In the story of *Dumbo*, many of the s_____ e_____ in the circus are c_____ and s_____ with their lives.	So, y'know the story of *Dumbo*? Well…many older elephants are really happy with their lives.
D_____ t____ p_____ associated with circuses, they r_____ a s_____ o____ e_____.	You see there're lots of problems with circuses? But everyone's like, "hey, they're fun!"
M_____, show producers have developed a l____ n____ o____ d____ e_____, with t_____ s____ a____ the Beatles, Christmas, or an action thriller.	Also, they've got tons of events for you. Like, you know, the Beatles, and Christmas, and, uh, like an action thriller.

Writing Outline: *Categorizing*

CD 1-25

Write about one type of entertainment that you know well for the school newsletter. What are some categories of this type of entertainment? Explain each category in detail.

Introduction	We all like entertainment. In my case, I love [entertainment type], but do you know anything about [category 1], [category 2], and [category 3]?
Category 1	[Category 1] is/are….
Category 2	As for [category 2],…
Category 3	Meanwhile, [category 3] is/are….
Summary	Now you know a bit about [categories 1, 2, and 3]. Join the chat online to share what you like!

UNIT 7 International Affairs

国際情勢について考えよう

Warm-up: *Share your ideas.*

What kinds of international affairs are you interested in?

a. Economic and trade relations.

b. Human rights and social issues.

c. Migration and refugee issues.

d. Environmental issues.

> *I chose answer _____ , because ....*
> ....
> ....
> ....

Words in Focus: *Search the internet for words and phrases.* 2-01

❏ Aleppo

❏ flee

❏ global citizen

❏ the Nobel Peace Prize

❏ PM2.5

❏ refugee

❏ SDGs

❏ the Taliban

❏ the UNHCR

❏ the Yazidi

SARJ blog

Student **A**ssociation for **R**efugees in **J**apan

Today, we are introducing the UNHCR Film Festival. Come join us and take this opportunity to learn more about the lives of [1]!

✔ *On Her Shoulders* (January 2018)

The 2018 Nobel Peace Prize winner, Nadia Murad, is a 23-year-old Yazidi. She escaped the sex slavery of the militant group ISIS. For the sake of women remaining in Northern Iraq, she shares information internationally on the reality that the Yazidis face. Eventually, she becomes the hope of the people.

✔ *Sonita* (October 2015)

Sonita flees from Afghanistan to Iran as a refugee to escape the Taliban. Her future dream is to be a rap musician, but women are not allowed [2] in Iran. Moreover, her parents order her to get married because they need money for her brother. Can Sonita seize the opportunity to change her life?

✔ *Last Men in Aleppo* (May 2017)

This award-winning documentary follows the three founding members of White Helmets. This organization was set up to save fellow citizens in the city of Aleppo during the Syrian Civil War. See how they face the dilemma of fleeing their country or staying and fighting for it.

✔ *Midnight Traveler* (September 2019)

Film director Hassan angered the Taliban because of his Afghan peace-themed film. Threats to his life [3] him to flee his hometown with his wife and two daughters. Hassan records the life-threatening journey of a wandering family in search of a safe place, with only a mobile phone in hand!

1. **Choose the best answer to complete the missing words in the passage.**

1. (A) film directors
   (B) militant groups
   (C) musicians
   (D) refugees

2. (A) sang
   (B) sing
   (C) singing
   (D) to sing

3. (A) faced
   (B) favored
   (C) forced
   (D) forgave

2. Read the passage and choose the best answer to each question.

1. What is the UNHCR Film Festival about?

(A) Learning about the lives of refugees.

(B) Participating in a sports tournament.

(C) Watching Hollywood movies.

(D) Attending a music festival.

2. Which movie involves a character whose actions are justified by a personal ambition?

(A) *On Her Shoulders*.

(B) *Last Men in Aleppo*.

(C) *Sonita*.

(D) *Midnight Traveler*.

3. Look at the chart. Which provides new information, not contained in the blog?

(A) The setting of *Sonita*.

(B) The characters in *Last Men in Aleppo*.

(C) The setting of *On Her Shoulders*.

(D) The characters in *Midnight Traveler*.

Movie Title	Setting	Characters
On Her Shoulders	Europe, North America	Nadia, trying to raise awareness of her country
Last Men in Aleppo	Syria	Members of the White Helmets
Sonita	Iran	Sonita, a wannabe rapper
Midnight Traveler	Afghanistan	Director and refugee Hassan

Reading Tips: *Sequencing*

英文の中で順序や時系列が入り組んでいる場合、整理して並べ替えることで事象の把握がスムーズになります。これを sequencing といいます。前ページの紹介文を元に 4 つの映画をリリース年ごとに並べ替え、地域に関連する情報をまとめましょう。

Year	Title	Area
2015	_____	Sonita flees from A_____ to I_____ as a refugee to escape the T_____.
2017	_____ _____	This organization was set up to save fellow citizens in the city of A_____ during the S_____ C_____ W_____.
2018	_____ _____	For the sake of women remaining in N_____ I_____, she shares information i_____ on the reality that the Y_____ face reality on i_____ f_____.
2019	_____	Film director Hassan angered the T_____ because of his A_____ peace-themed film.

Global environment

Last week, I participated in an online international conference on the global environment. We mainly discussed SDGs 3, 13, and 14. The SDGs are the Sustainable Development Goals, a universal call by the United Nations. At first, I thought these goals were to help poor people in specific countries. Later, I realized that they are related to every
5　human life, including mine, in the whole world.

We started the conference with the topics related to SDG 3. A Chinese student told us that China has been facing serious air pollution caused by PM2.5. When she mentioned PM2.5, I was suddenly scared because I had heard that it was also a problem in Japan. These
10　tiny particles **spread** across national borders, pollute our air, and threaten our lives. We had a short coffee break after this discussion, and I had a friendly conversation with the Chinese student.

After the coffee break, a researcher from Australia showed us a figure. It showed that
15　climate change (SDG 13) is affecting the distribution of plants and animals on Earth. With global warming, the **habitats** of plants and animals are moving to cooler places, which leads to changes in ecosystems. Though the change also affects human life, we humans are not just victims. I had mixed feelings when I learned that human activities themselves are causing global warming.
20

In the end, in relation to SDG 14, a participant from India said marine pollution in the Indian Ocean is serious. I told her that Japan is also facing marine pollution from plastic waste, industrial oil, and chemicals. When we looked at a map, we found that **pollutants** float and arrive in any country regardless of their border lines. I realized that no one country's
25　policies alone can stop dangerous **substances** from polluting our oceans.

When I decided to attend this conference, I thought it would be great to meet people online across borders. Through this conference, I realized that environmental issues also **transcend** national borders. No matter where we live, the issues we have are connected to
30　each other. As a global citizen, I would like to continue exchanging information on such international issues.

Your Reading Speed: **360** words ÷ _____ seconds × 60 = _____ wpm

1. **Choose the phrase that is related to each word / phrase.**

1. spread   (   )

2. habitat   (   )

3. pollutant   (   )

4. substance   (   )

5. transcend   (   )

(a) a harmful material in the environment
(b) material with specific characteristics
(c) natural environment where animals live and grow
(d) to extend and cover a larger area
(e) to rise above limitations or boundaries

2. **Read the passage and choose the best answer to each question.**

1. What are the SDGs?
   (A) Online conferences on the global environment.
   (B) Conferences for developed countries.
   (C) Goals related to life in the whole world.
   (D) Goals to help poor people in specific countries.

2. What was the topic of discussion related to SDG 3 at the conference?
   (A) Water pollution in Africa.
   (B) Air pollution in China.
   (C) Deforestation in South America.
   (D) Soil pollution in Europe.

3. What did the figure presented by the Australian researcher show?
   (A) The growth of the global population.
   (B) The effect of natural disasters on ecosystems.
   (C) The relationship between air pollution and human health.
   (D) The impact of climate change on the distribution of plants and animals.

4. What was the topic of discussion related to SDG 14 at the conference?
   (A) The impact of climate change on marine life.
   (B) The overfishing in the Atlantic Ocean.
   (C) The effect of sea level rises on coastal cities.
   (D) The problem of marine pollution in the Indian Ocean.

5. What did the speaker realize about environmental issues?
   (A) They do not affect people across national borders.
   (B) They only affect people who live in specific regions.
   (C) They are connected to each other regardless of where we live.
   (D) They are only a concern for a few countries.

Writing Tips: *Narrative essay*

Narrative essay では、ある出来事 (もしくは複数の連続した出来事) が時系列順にどのように起こったかを伝えます。筆者が経験したことに重点を置き、I, my などの一人称を使います。40 ページの文章の構成をまとめてみましょう。

Outline	Example
Catchy Introduction	Last week, I p_____ in an o_____ i_____ c_____ on the g_____ e_____ .
Beginning	We s_____ the c_____ with the topics r_____ to S___ ____ .
Middle	A_____ the c_____ b_____ , a researcher from Australia showed us a figure.
End	In the e____ , in relation to SDG 14, a participant from India said m_____ p_____ in the I_____ O_____ is s_____ .
Conclusion	As a global citizen, I would like to c_____ e_____ i_____ on s____ i_____ i____ .

Writing Outline: *Sequencing*

Tell a story about a time when you learned something about international affairs. Include a catchy introduction, beginning, middle, end, and conclusion.

Introduction	[Catchy introduction]. I learned this during [time/event]. [Background information].
Beginning	When I was....
Middle	Then, when I....
End	In the end,....
Conclusion	In conclusion, after this experience I realized that....

Technology

身近にある科学技術について考えよう

What comes to mind when you think of "technology"?

a. Artificial intelligence and robots.

b. Digital tools and software.

c. Convenience and accessibility.

d. Things that are hard to understand.

I chose answer _____ , because ….

....
....
....

❏ alternative

❏ electric vehicle

❏ epidemic infectious disease

❏ navigate

❏ online class

❏ poor connection

❏ pros and cons

❏ resume

❏ technological innovation

❏ Wi-Fi system

✏️ **Teacher** 15:30	**# Face to face lessons # Real-time online classes # Education** Hi everyone! Today's topic is "real-time online lessons." Do you think they are a good type of lesson for Japanese students studying English?
👧 **Ruby** 15:38	To [**1**] the risk of epidemic infectious diseases, real-time online lessons provide a safer alternative for students to have lessons at the same time, thanks to technology!
👦 **Ken** 15:55	@**Ruby:** You've got a point there, but online classes create an economic burden for the learners. Students need a computer, Wi-Fi system, and other accessories.
👩 **Sara** 15:57	@**Ken:** I agree. Also, there may be technical problems like being disconnected from the classes by a poor connection. Not every student can work well by accessing a class on time in perfect conditions.
😀 **Eric** 16:04	@**Ken** @**Sara:** Although real-time online lessons have disadvantages, they could be a helpful learning method to [**2**] students' stress from studying English. Some students feel nervous when they make presentations face to face. Having lessons via a screen creates a more relaxed atmosphere for using English. Students may work even better to express their opinions in English by using functions like the "chat box" or "discussion room."
👩 **Mari** 16:10	@**Eric:** I understand what you're saying, but it may be hard to keep students' attention. A teacher cannot check every student's facial expression and reaction at once from a screen. On the other hand, students may get tired or not focus on a lesson if they have to watch a screen for 90 minutes.
✏️ **Teacher** 16:57	Thanks for your opinions! All in all, real-time online lessons could be a [**3**] way for Japanese students to learn English. However, they are unlikely to completely replace face-to-face lessons. Any other comments?

1. **Choose the best answer to complete the missing words in the passage.**

1. (A) decreasing	**2.** (A) less	**3.** (A) suited
(B) decrease	(B) lessen	(B) suit
(C) decreased	(C) lesson	(C) suitable
(D) be decreased	(D) lesser	(D) soothed

2. **Read the passage and choose the best answer to each question.**

1. Who has a positive opinion about real-time online classes?
   (A) Ruby and Ken.
   (B) Ken and Sara.
   (C) Sara and Eric.
   (D) Ruby and Eric.

2. What is the opinion of the teacher about real-time online classes?
   (A) They can replace face-to-face lessons.
   (B) They are a bad way of teaching English.
   (C) They are the only way of teaching English.
   (D) They are one way of teaching English.

3. Look at the display. Who is worried about this kind of problem during the class?
   (A) Ruby.　(B) Ken.　(C) Sara.　(D) Eric.

Poor Connection

The video will resume automatically when the connection improves.

Reading Tips: *Comparison and contrast*

複数のものを比較して類似点や相違点を分析することは comparison、対比して相違点を明確にすることは contrast と呼ばれます。以下の表では、前ページの投稿者がそれぞれの項目に関して触れていれば✔印を記入した上で、最後の行にオンライン授業に賛成しているか反対しているかを選び、5人の意見を比べましょう。

	Ruby	Ken	Sara	Eric	Mari
Avoid infection					
Economic burden					
Technical problems					
Relaxed atmosphere					
Online functions					
Keep attention					
Agree with online classes?	Yes / No	Yes / No	Yes / No	Yes / No	Yes / No

Academic Reading
Change your car, change the world!

EC CD 2-07

Drive into the future!

One technological **innovation** which changed the shape of the 20th century was the motor car. In the 21st century, cars are essential for families in much of the developed world, but problems have emerged. Our planet is being destroyed by human demands for luxury and convenience. Although people are reluctant to stop using private vehicles for transportation, there are now safer choices.

First, it is no longer necessary to buy a car that uses gasoline. This fuel is responsible for around 20% of damage to the global environment. Unfortunately, **approximately** 80% of cars sold in the world today rely on gasoline (Statista, 2023). However, electric cars, which have been available since 1890, are much cleaner with lower fuel costs. Hybrid options are also available and popular in Japan, where it is still difficult to find charging points for electric cars.

Second, technological progress means that in the future, people may not need to drive at all. Self-driving cars will transport passengers, navigate routes, control speeds, and follow safety rules automatically. Accidents have happened, but technology is **constantly** improving, and such vehicles are now safer than the average human driver (United States Department of Transportation, n.d.). In the coming years, cars will be controlled by machines, not by humans.

The above changes point to a new world for transportation. One likely development is that people will not need to buy cars at all. Instead, they will be able to call up a car using a phone application. This is different from a taxi service, because there is no driver and costs are lower. After reaching the destination, the car returns to base, avoiding parking fees. Gasoline is not needed, so the environmental impact will be much lower than it is today. Such a future might **resemble** a sci-fi movie, but the benefits are many.

Today, much of the world **revolves around** the ownership of private cars. Now that we are experiencing the damaging effects of vehicle pollution, urgent changes are needed. The priority for car manufacturers and owners is a shift to electric vehicles. In addition to that, the adoption of self-driving cars will make roads safer, cheaper, and more accessible. This will allow car passengers to sit back, relax, and watch a revolution on the road.

Your Reading Speed: **380** words ÷ ________ seconds × 60 = ________ wpm

References

Statista (2023). *Breakdown of global car sales in 2019 and 2030, by fuel technology*. https://www.statista.com/statistics/827460/global-car-sales-by-fuel-technology/

United States Department of Transportation (n.d.). *Automated Driving Systems*. National Highway Traffic Safety Administration. https://www.nhtsa.gov/vehicle-manufacturers/automated-driving-systems

1. **Choose the phrase that is related to each word / phrase.**

    1. innovation   (   )
    2. approximately   (   )
    3. constantly   (   )
    4. resemble   (   )
    5. revolve around   (   )

    (a) about, around
    (b) always
    (c) development, invention
    (d) seem like
    (e) to center on

2. **Read the passage and choose the best answer to each question.**

    1. According to the first paragraph, what is a problem with cars?
    (A) Families don't need them.
    (B) They harm the Earth.
    (C) They are not convenient enough.
    (D) They are a safe choice.

    2. Which is not true about electric cars?
    (A) They are a recent development.
    (B) They are relatively clean.
    (C) Fuel costs are lower.
    (D) It is not easy to charge them in Japan.

    3. Which of the following is an advantage of self-driving cars?
    (A) They can travel quickly.
    (B) They are relatively safe.
    (C) There are no accidents.
    (D) People do not need them.

    4. In what way will future cars be different from taxi services?
    (A) Everyone will start buying them.
    (B) Drivers will pay the parking fees.
    (C) Passengers can watch a movie.
    (D) Future cars will be cheaper.

    5. Which does the writer suggest people consider first?
    (A) Private vehicles.
    (B) Hybrid vehicles.
    (C) Electric vehicles.
    (D) Self-driving vehicles.

Writing Tips: *Persuasive essay*

説得型エッセイ (persuasive essay) は、書き手の考えを読み手に理解させ、書き手の議論 (argument) に妥当性があると納得させるエッセイです。したがって、"It depends" のような、主張を弱める表現は避けなければなりません。以下の構成に沿って、説得型エッセイの構成をまとめましょう。

Outline	Example
Introduce your argument	Although people are reluctant to stop using private vehicles for transportation, t_____ a____ n____ s_____ c_____.
Reason 1	First, it is n____ l_____ n_____ t____ b____ a car t_____ u____ g_____.
Reason 1 example	This fuel is responsible for a_____ ____% of d_____ t____ t____ g____ e_____.
Reason 2	Second, t_____ p_____ means that in the future, p____ m____ n____ n____ t____ d_____ at all.
Reason 2 example	Self-driving cars will t_____ p_____, n____ r_____, c____ s_____, and f____ s_____ r_____ a_____.
Conclusion	The above changes p_____ t_____ a n____ w_____ f_____ t_____.

Writing Outline: *Giving an example and reasons*

 2-08

Write about one example of new technology that you are excited about. Give an example of how this technology is used, and give two reasons why you like it.

Introduction	I would like to talk about [type of new technology] as an example of new technology.
Example	One good example is.... This is....
Reason 1	One thing I love about this technology is....
Reason 2	Another great thing is....
Conclusion	In conclusion,....

My Future

将来の自分について考えよう

Warm-up: *Share your ideas.*

When you hear the word "future," what do you imagine?

a. After my graduation.

b. After my retirement.

c. The future of my children.

d. The future of the Earth.

I chose answer _____ , because ....

Words in Focus: *Search the internet for words and phrases.* 2-09

❏ determinant

❏ fortune teller

❏ futurism

❏ Gallup World Poll

❏ GDP

❏ life expectancy

❏ outcome

❏ short-term goal

❏ well-being

❏ the World Happiness Report

Word of the Day : Jun 22

futurist noun [C] /ˈfjuːtʃərˌɪst/

1. **(EXPERT)** a person who makes statements about what will happen in the future based on their studies and knowledge
2. **(ARTIST)** a supporter of futurism or an artist who uses a futurist style

Cambridge Advanced Learner's Dictionary

When you saw the word "futurist," did you imagine a mysterious fortune teller? Not exactly. Futurists are like paid 　1　 who use facts, trends, and current realities to see what kind of future outcomes could be possible.

How can we think like a futurist? Usually, we are good at making "short-term" goals, like what to do today. This focus on the short-term can be a 　2　. For example, companies may not want to spend money on rebuilding old infrastructure. Instead, they may want to participate in a new construction project. However, futurists think about "long-term" goals. They would advise companies to fix the older bridges, because they predict these buildings would fall apart in 10 or 20 years.

So how should we think about the future? We often think about what happens between the moment we are born and the day we pass away. Instead, futurists expand the image of the future to other generations. Let's take another example. You are babysitting a five-year-old. He is crying because he wants a piece of candy. Would you just give it to him to stop him crying? Or, you might patiently tell him why he cannot get this candy now. This would definitely take 　3　 time than the short-term solution but could affect how this child might interact with his own children in the future.

1. **Choose the best answer to complete the missing words in the passage.**

1. (A) accountants
   (B) consultants
   (C) designers
   (D) pharmacists

2. (A) problem
   (B) product
   (C) profit
   (D) progress

3. (A) few
   (B) less
   (C) many
   (D) more

2. **Read the passage and choose the best answer to each question.**

1. If you think like a futurist, you would...
   (A) focus on what to do today.
   (B) rebuild old bridges.
   (C) participate in a new project.
   (D) destroy the bridges now.

2. Which of the following is most important for futurists?
   (A) To stop a child from crying.
   (B) To provide children with enough food.
   (C) To teach children how precious time is.
   (D) To discipline children for their future.

3. Look at Ken's note. Which of his goals are short-term?
   (A) #1 and #2.
   (B) #2 and #3.
   (C) #3 and #4.
   (D) #4 and #1.

My Goals   Ken

#1. Improve people's work styles in Japan
#2. Succeed in the global market
#3. Choose which business seminar to join
#4. Visit a tennis club and make friends

Reading Tips: *Main idea and details (2)*

前ページの記事では、それぞれの段落の冒頭で topic sentence が疑問文で提示されています。そして、第2・第3段落では、身近な例を挙げて topic sentence に対する詳しい説明をしています。どのような例が挙げられているか書き出して整理しましょう。

Paragraph	Topic sentence	Example
2	H____ can we t_____ l____ a f_____ ?	F____ e_____, c_____ m__ n__ w____ to s_____ m_____ on rebuilding old infrastructure.
3	So h____ should we t_____ a_____ the f_____ ?	Let's take a_____ e_____. You are b_____ a five-year-old. He is c_____ because he w_____ a p_____ of c_____.

The World Happiness Report

Every year, the World Happiness Report ranks over 150 countries by how happy their citizens feel. Nordic countries such as Finland and Denmark are always listed in the top ten happiest countries (Helliwell et al., 2022). Does this mean that you should move to Finland to live a happy future? In this essay, the results of this report will be examined by focusing on
5   three points: data bias, **subjective** well-being, and ways to measure happiness.

First, the World Happiness Report does not cover every single country. For example, it is unknown how Cubans feel about their happiness because Cuba does not **appear** in the report. Also, data from some countries is incomplete. The report generally summarizes
10   three years of survey responses for around 1,000 people per country per year. However, in particular, Jamaica's data represents only 504 responses gathered in one year. Data with a small number of samples may be biased.

Secondly, the happiness scores are taken from the individuals' own assessments,
15   indicated by the Gallup World Poll. Participants are asked to imagine a ladder with steps numbered from 0 (the worst possible life) to 10 (the best possible life). They then answer which step of the ladder they are standing on. The lowest and highest measures of assessment are set by individuals, which means the measures are very **subjective**. Also, **modest** people tend to avoid extreme scores like 0 and 10.
20

Third, there should be numerous factors that bring about happiness. However, the happiness ranking is calculated by six determinants: GDP per person, healthy life expectancy, social support, perceived freedom to make life choices, **generosity**, and perception of corruption. In the FAQ section of the World Happiness Report, it says "(s)ome important
25   variables, such as unemployment or inequality, do not appear because comparable international data are not yet available for the full sample of countries."

Looking at the **superficial** rankings alone, people in one country seem to be more or less happy than those in other countries. However, the results can be affected by how the data is
30   gathered. After all, happiness is a **subjective** feeling and should vary from person to person. Rather than judging people by rankings, it is important to look at the data in detail and investigate how all the people around the world can enjoy happiness.

> Your Reading Speed: **387** words ÷ _____ seconds × 60 = _____ wpm

Reference
Helliwell, J. F., Layard, R., Sachs, J. D., De Neve, J. E., Aknin, L. B., & Wang, S. (Eds.). (2022). *World Happiness Report 2022*. Sustainable Development Solutions Network.

1. Choose the phrase that is related to each word / phrase.

1. subjective   (   )
2. appear   (   )
3. modest   (   )
4. generosity   (   )
5. superficial   (   )

(a) from the perspective of individual(s)
(b) giving freely and kindly
(c) humble
(d) surface
(e) to be seen

2. Read the passage and choose the best answer to each question.

1. Which of the following does this essay examine?
   (A) How many countries there are in the world.
   (B) Problems that Nordic countries have.
   (C) Methods to figure out how happy people are.
   (D) How to make people in Finland happy.

2. What is a limitation of the World Happiness Report?
   (A) It covers every country in the world.
   (B) It includes data from a large sample of people.
   (C) It reports the happiness levels of Cuban citizens.
   (D) It has missing or incomplete data from some countries.

3. What does it mean when a survey participant answers "7"?
   (A) The happiest ever.
   (B) Rather happy.
   (C) Rather unhappy.
   (D) The most unhappy.

4. Which one is included in the six factors?
   (A) Economic situation.
   (B) Education system.
   (C) Gender equality.
   (D) Unemployment rate.

5. What does the author recommend in order to understand happiness better?
   (A) Relying on superficial rankings alone.
   (B) Comparing happiness across different countries.
   (C) Investigating data in detail.
   (D) Judging people by rankings.

Writing Tips: *APA (2) In-text citations*

他の人が書いた文章を自分の文章の中で使用する際には、引用元となった文献を in-text citation として明確に示す必要があります。APA スタイルでは通常 (著者名 , 出版年) もしくは (組織名 , 出版年) のように表記します。52 ページの文章で引用されている文献が、どのように表記されているか書き出しましょう。

Reference	In-text citation
H_____, J. F., L_____, R., S_____, J. D., D___ N___, J. E., A_____, L. B., & W_____, S. (Eds.). (2022). *W_____ H_____ R____ 2____*. Sustainable Development Solutions Network.	(H_____ et al., 2022)

* 注 :" et al." は 3 人以上の著者がいる参考文献で使用します。In-text citation で見られる通り、第一著者名の後に et al. を記して引用します。

Writing Outline: *Main idea and details (2)*

What is one big change that will happen in the near future? Explain the change in detail. Include at least one reference.

Introduction	One thing that is likely to change in __ years is…. I will describe this change in detail.
Detail 1: "What"	This change means that….
Detail 2: "When"	According to [Author (year)], this change will happen….
Detail 3: "Why"	The main reason(s) for this change is/are….
Conclusion	In conclusion, [change] will happen [**when**] because [**why**]….
References	

UNIT 10 Personal Finance

お金の管理について考えよう

Warm-up: *Share your ideas.*

What is the best way to grow your money?

a. Buying lottery tickets.

b. Putting money in a savings account.

c. Investing in stocks.

d. Starting a small business.

I chose answer _____ , because ....

....

....

....

Words in Focus: *Search the internet for words and phrases.* 2-13

❏ compound interest

❏ deposit

❏ finance

❏ fraud

❏ interest rate

❏ piggy bank

❏ principal

❏ refund

❏ savings account

❏ scheme

Talking about money is not taboo.

 2-14

WORLDWIDE BANK

How Much Can You Save for Your Retirement?

How much do you make per month? How do you spend your money? How much do you have in your savings account? According to the Japanese government, people need to save around 20 million yen to secure their life after retirement. How much can you save for your retirement? Suppose that you [__1__] in the workforce for the next 40 years.

There are various ways to save money. Here, let's compare two ways, using a traditional piggy bank versus a savings account. For example, put ¥10,000 per month in the piggy bank. In this way, you will save ¥4.8 million by the time you retire. Or [__2__] ¥10,000 per month at 1% annual interest in the savings account. This time, you will get a deposit of nearly ¥5.9 million (before tax) by the age of retirement. In both cases, the monthly deposit and length of time are the same. Nevertheless, you will get around one million yen more in the latter case!

Why is that? The difference between these is only whether or not you have [__3__]. In particular, compound interest makes the principal (the initial amount of money) grow enormously. It is also called interest on interest over the investment period. The main factors of compound interest are principal, interest rate, frequency, and the period you keep your money in the bank. Among them, the most significant factor is the period which makes the principal increase.

In general, talking about money may not be an appropriate topic in Japanese society. However, it is important to know how to manage your personal finances. There are various ways to save money, such as through saving, investment, or insurance to establish a successful life. Why not start saving for retirement right now?

---

1. Choose the best answer to complete the missing words in the passage.

1. (A) had been
   (B) was
   (C) being
   (D) will be

2. (A) deposit
   (B) donate
   (C) inherit
   (D) withdraw

3. (A) insurance
   (B) interest
   (C) investment
   (D) incentive

2. Read the passage and choose the best answer to each question.

1. Which of the following does the writer mention?

    (A) The amount of money in a savings account.

    (B) How to spend 20 million yen.

    (C) How to earn interest from a piggy bank.

    (D) The amount of money to withdraw every month.

2. Look at the chart. What does it explain?

    (A) Retirement age.

    (B) Piggy bank investment.

    (C) The compound interest system.

    (D) None of the above.

3. What does the writer suggest at the end?

    (A) Don't talk about money in Japan.

    (B) Investing is the best way to save money.

    (C) Personal finance management is important.

    (D) Don't start saving for retirement yet.

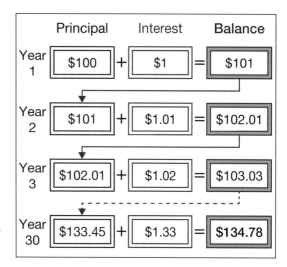

Reading Tips: *Inference (1)*

Inference とは、文中でどのようなことが示唆されているかを推測して論じることです。以下は、前ページの英文の各段落からの推論を示したものです。どの文からの推論なのかを探して、書き出しましょう。

Paragraph	Sentence	推論
1	According to the Japanese government, people need to s___ a_____ ____m___ y___ to secure their life after retirement.	自分の稼ぎでは老後の蓄えが足りないかもしれない
2	Nevertheless, you will g____ a_____ o___ m_____ y___ m___ i___ t___ l___ c____!	預金口座に預ける方が得をするかもしれない
3	Among them, t___ m___ s_____ f____ i___ t___ p____ which makes the principal increase.	早い時期から始める方が得をするかもしれない
4	There are various ways to save money, such as through s_____, i_____, o___ i_____ to establish a successful life.	個人資産の管理方法は他にもあるかもしれない

Ponzi, pyramid, and new types of schemes

Everyone wants to earn, save, and spend money efficiently. However, trying to make a lot of money with little effort can easily make you a victim of **fraud**. This essay introduces classic methods such as Ponzi and pyramid schemes, as well as **fraud** schemes that have become a problem in recent years.

5

The Ponzi scheme was named after Charles Ponzi, a scammer in the early 1990s. He explained to the investors that they could profit from the difference in the exchange rates of international postage coupons and those of foreign **currencies**. However, he only bought a small number of postage coupons. Most of the money he returned to the earlier investors

10 came straight from the newer investors. Thus, in the Ponzi scheme, the collected money does not make any profit. It eventually fails as people stop investing their money or start asking for a full refund.

In pyramid schemes, just like the peak of a pyramid, the top layer of the **hierarchy**

15 starts with a small number of members. Those people recruit new members who belong to the second layer. Thus, this model creates a chain of participants. New members usually pay a participation fee or buy goods or services. Those in the upper layers can supposedly benefit from the money gained by those in the lower layers. However, a simple calculation proves that this model always collapses. If each participant needs to recruit six members to gain profit, the

20 number of new participants exceeds the world's population before the 13th layer.

New types of similar schemes have emerged one after another, using different tricks to **exploit** human greed. They are promoted through business or investment seminars, networking parties, bargain offers, and many other forms. On the internet, pages that contain

25 advice on how to avoid **fraud** may be operated by **fraud** groups. Regardless of how these schemes are promoted and managed, the scammers argue that their business models are completely new and unconventional, and of course, legal.

One way to deal with such schemes is to imagine why those people want to tell others

30 their secrets about such easy and efficient ways of making money. Essentially, money is something that can be earned after certain effort and labor. Any business model that gives the illusion that money automatically produces money should be considered **suspicious**.

Your Reading Speed: **393** words ÷ _____ seconds × 60 = _____ wpm

1. **Choose the phrase that is related to each word / phrase.**

1. fraud ( )
2. currency ( )
3. hierarchy ( )
4. exploit ( )
5. suspicious ( )

(a) crime of cheating people
(b) doubtful
(c) ranking order
(d) system of money in use
(e) to take unfair advantage

2. **Read the passage and choose the best answer to each question.**

1. What does the essay warn against?
   (A) Trying to make a lot of money with little effort.
   (B) Saving money effectively.
   (C) Investing money in reliable stocks.
   (D) Following financial experts.

2. What did Charles Ponzi do?
   (A) He invited people to invest money.
   (B) He bought too many postage coupons.
   (C) He worked in a foreign bank.
   (D) He asked for a full refund.

3. How do pyramid schemes work?
   (A) Participants work for travel agencies.
   (B) Participants pay a participation fee.
   (C) Participants survey the pyramid.
   (D) Participants calculate the world's population.

4. How do the scammers usually describe their business models?
   (A) New and unconventional, and illegal.
   (B) Old and conventional, and legal.
   (C) New and unconventional, and legal.
   (D) Old and conventional, and illegal.

5. What does the author suggest?
   (A) Respect your business teacher.
   (B) Tell people your secret.
   (C) Use the Ponzi scheme to earn money.
   (D) Beware of advice about easy money.

Writing Tips: *What is a good thesis statement?*

Thesis statement とは、自分がエッセイで伝えたい主張を簡潔にまとめて最初のパラグラフに書くものです。以下は、58 ページの文章の各パラグラフ最初の 1 文を抜き出したものです。Thesis statement がどう書かれているかに注目しながら下線部を埋めましょう。

Thesis statement	This essay introduces c_____ m_____ such as P_____ and p_____ s_____, as well as f_____ s_____ that have become a problem in r_____ y_____.
Paragraph 2	The P_____ s_____ was named after Charles Ponzi, a s_____ i____ t____ e____ 1_____.
Paragraph 3	In pyramid schemes, just like the p_____ o___ a p_____, the t___ l_____ of the hierarchy starts with a s_____ n___ o___ m_____.
Paragraph 4	N____ t_____ o___ s_____ s_____ have emerged one after another, using different t____ t____ e____ h____ g_____.
Conclusion	One way to deal with such schemes is to i_____ w___ t_____ p____ w____ t____ t____ o____ t_____ s_____ about such easy and efficient ways of making money.

Writing Outline: *Inference (1)*

Find some financial advice online. What does the advice say, and what can you infer from it?

Thesis statement	A lot of advice on [topic] is available online. [Thesis statement].
Advice	According to [Author (year)],....
Inference 1	What I understood from this is....
Inference 2	This advice also suggests that....
Conclusion	[Author (year)] advises [advice]. For me, this means [inference 1] and [inference 2].

UNIT 11

Health

心と体の健康について考えよう

Warm-up: *Share your ideas.*

Which of the following health issues are you concerned about most?

a. Nutrition and diet.

b. Pandemic preparedness.

c. Mental health.

d. Emergency medical services.

I chose answer _____ , because ....
....
....
....

Words in Focus: *Search the internet for words and phrases.* 2-17

❏ allergic reaction

❏ diagnose

❏ dizziness

❏ heart attack

❏ medical emergency

❏ overdose

❏ paralysis

❏ seizure

❏ stroke

❏ vaccine

Symptoms of life-threatening conditions

In the event of an accident or sudden illness, we get anxious and panic.
Should you go to the hospital on your own or call an ambulance?
If you are not sure, first consider whether the situation is life-threatening.
If it is, it's time to call an ambulance.
Here are some examples of life-threatening conditions that require an ambulance.

The patient may have had a stroke if you see the following symptoms.
✓ Sudden paralysis, numbness, or weakness of the face, arm, or leg.
✓ Sudden confusion, trouble with speaking, swallowing, or understanding.
✓ Sudden trouble with ⎡ **1** ⎤ in one or both eyes.
✓ Sudden trouble with walking, dizziness or loss of balance or coordination.
✓ Sudden severe headache with no known cause.

The patient may be suffering a heart attack if you see the following symptoms.
✓ Chest pain or discomfort.
✓ Feeling weak, light-headed, or faint.
✓ Pain or discomfort in the jaw, neck, or back.
✓ Pain or discomfort in one or ⎡ **2** ⎤ arms, or shoulders.
✓ Shortness of breath.

Other symptoms to be concerned about are as follows.
✓ Not responding at all or appropriately.
✓ Having a seizure.
✓ Shortness of breath or difficulty breathing.
✓ Bleeding uncontrollably.
✓ Having a severe allergic reaction.
✓ Severe burns.
✓ Swallowing something poisonous.
✓ Having thoughts of hurting themselves or others.
✓ Intentional or ⎡ **3** ⎤ drug overdose.

1. **Choose the best answer to complete the missing words in the passage.**

1. (A) see	**2.** (A) any	**3.** (A) accident
(B) saw	(B) both	(B) accidents
(C) seen	(C) each	(C) accidental
(D) seeing	(D) every	(D) accidentally

2. Read the passage and choose the best answer to each question.

1. What should you do if somebody is in a life-threatening condition?
   (A) Call a friend.
   (B) Go to the hospital on your own.
   (C) Call an ambulance.
   (D) Wait for the symptoms to disappear.

2. Which of the following can be a symptom of a heart attack?
   (A) Your legs suddenly go numb.
   (B) You feel something wrong in your back.
   (C) The bleeding does not stop.
   (D) You are severely burned.

3. Look at the memo on the right. What information do you need to give on the emergency call?
   (A) The hospital location.
   (B) The number to call an ambulance.
   (C) The doctor's name.
   (D) The patient's condition.

memo

Questions you will be asked in medical emergency calls.

☐ Where is the patient?
☐ What number are you calling from?
☐ What is your name?
☐ What happened exactly?
☐ How old is the patient?
☐ Is the patient conscious?
☐ Is the patient breathing?

Reading Tips: *Inference (2)*

Inference には、本文の内容を自分なりに咀嚼して考えるリーディング技術が必要とされます。前ページの文章をもとに、以下の内容が示唆されているかどうかを考えてみましょう。

What can be inferred about a medical emergency?	Yes / No?
(1) When you get anxious and panic, you should request an ambulance.	
(2) A sudden onset of serious symptoms could indicate a stroke.	
(3) Shortness of breath is the only symptom of a heart attack.	
(4) You should call an ambulance when you can't stop harming yourself.	

Emergency SOS in London and around the world

It was Friday morning. The night before, I had a party with my Japanese friends at my dorm in London, and we all fell asleep. We woke up to one of our friends **moaning** about having a headache. After a while, he lost consciousness. We called 119 and asked for an ambulance. It would have been the right thing to do if we were in Japan. However, to our surprise, the call led to a COVID-19 testing and vaccine helpline.

5

I explained to the operator that my friend was **unconscious**. He then told me to dial 999, the number for serious medical emergencies. I later discovered that Cambodia, South Korea, and Taiwan are the countries where you can call 119 to request an ambulance, just like in Japan. In China, on the other hand, 119 is used to report fires. For ambulance services in China, dial 120. Other emergency numbers are 911 in the US and Canada, 000 in Australia, and 111 in New Zealand.

10

Anyway, I **hurriedly** called 999. When the call went through, I was already panicking, and all I could do was shout, "Help!" The operator said something, but I couldn't understand it, so I asked my friend Ken to take over the phone. I later found out that the operator was saying, "Police, fire, or ambulance?" In Japan, 119 leads to fire and ambulance calls, while in the UK, 999 leads to a center that also includes the police.

15

Well, Ken did a great job telling the operator about our friend's condition. Ken was asked if we wanted to go to the hospital on our own. The operator said, "Arriving by ambulance does not always mean you'll see the doctor sooner than if you had walked in." We still chose to have the ambulance come, but it felt like hours before we finally heard the ambulance **sirens**.

20

25

The friend we took to the hospital was diagnosed with a stroke. After that incident, Ken and I learned a lot about medical emergencies abroad. For example, there are few countries where we can ride ambulances for free. However, this is what we found out in the spring of 2023, so the medical system in each region may change. Whenever I travel to any country in the future, I should get the latest information **ahead of time** and prepare for emergencies.

30

Your Reading Speed: **400** words ÷ _____ seconds × 60 = _____ wpm

1. Choose the phrase that is related to each word / phrase.

1. moan ( )
2. unconscious ( )
3. hurriedly ( )
4. siren ( )
5. ahead of time ( )

(a) beforehand
(b) loud, high-pitched warning signal
(c) not responding to surroundings
(d) quickly
(e) to make a low sound expressing pain

2. Read the passage and choose the best answer to each question.

1. What did the author do first when their friend lost consciousness?
   (A) Took their friend to his dormitory.
   (B) Talked to an ambulance driver.
   (C) Called a COVID-19 testing and vaccine helpline.
   (D) Took their friend to the hospital.

2. Which number should you dial to request a fire engine in China?
   (A) 999.
   (B) 119.
   (C) 120.
   (D) 911.

3. What did the operator want to know when the author called 999?
   (A) The name of the patient.
   (B) How to calm Ken down.
   (C) The type of emergency.
   (D) Where the patient was.

4. What did the operator suggest on the phone?
   (A) They should drive to the hospital on their own.
   (B) They may have to wait even if they call an ambulance.
   (C) They may have to walk to the hospital.
   (D) They should wait hours before the ambulance arrives.

5. What did the author learn after taking their sick friend to the hospital?
   (A) How to diagnose a stroke.
   (B) Medical emergency systems are the same in every country.
   (C) Few countries provide free ambulance services.
   (D) Emergency preparedness is unnecessary when traveling.

Writing Tips: *Self-reflective writing*

Self-reflective writing は、自分の行動、体験、考えていた事などを振り返るために書くもので、日記なども含みます。64 ページの文章の構成をまとめてみましょう。

Outline	Example
Situation	It was F_____ m_____. The night before, I had a p_____ w___ m___ J_____ f_____ a___ m___ d_____ i____ L_____, and we all fell asleep.
Detail	We woke up to o____ o____ o____ f_____ m_____ a_____ h_____ ____ h_____. After a while, h___ l_____ c_____.
Reflection	We still chose to h____ t____ a_____ c_____, but it f_____ l_____ h_____ before we finally heard the ambulance sirens.
Conclusion	Whenever I travel to any country in the future, I should g_____ t____ l_____ i_____ ahead of time and p_____ f___ e_____.

Writing Outline: *Inference (2)*

 2-20

Write about a health problem that you have experienced. What advice is available online? What can you infer from it? Reflect on your own experience.

Introduction	When I.... [time] I suffered from [health problem]. I would like to share some advice I found and what this means to me.
Online advice	According to [Author (year)],....
Inference	What I understood from this is....
Self-reflection	Personally, I feel that....
Conclusion	To sum up, one solution for [health problem] is [**online advice**]. In my view....

Diversity

多様性について考えよう

Warm-up: *Share your ideas.*

Which best describes the area where you live?

   a. There are people with various backgrounds.

   b. Most people look similar.

   c. Most of the residents are elderly.

   d. There are people of all ages.

I chose answer _____ , because ....
....
....
....

Words in Focus: *Search the internet for words and phrases.* 2-21

- ❏ affirmative action
- ❏ the Civil Rights Act
- ❏ compensation
- ❏ ethnic group
- ❏ racial quota

- ❏ racist
- ❏ Romani
- ❏ unconscious bias
- ❏ the US Supreme Court
- ❏ xenophobia

What is xenophobia?

Have you ever heard of xenophobia? This means a dislike or [1] of people and things which are foreign or strange. For example, some people might complain that there are too many foreigners in their country. Is this a natural thing to say? Or perhaps a company you know pays lower wages to foreign workers. Do you think that is fair? Actually, these are both examples of xenophobia.

Xenophobia is an extremely serious problem. Before he became leader of Germany, Adolf Hitler had developed a dislike for several groups in German society. In particular, he held a deep hatred for Jewish people. These feelings were based on old teachings. In addition, he strongly disliked Romani and Black people. These views influenced Hitler's period as German leader in a most [2] way.

In 1935, Hitler's Nazi party announced laws to stop German people from having relationships with Jewish, Romani, and Black people. In the 1940s, the Nazis murdered six million Jews, around two-thirds of the population of Jewish people in Europe. They were caught and taken away to be murdered. Very few Jews survived in Nazi-controlled land.

Xenophobia still causes problems around the world today. In 2015, Zimbabweans living in South Africa were attacked and killed by people who wanted them to leave the country. In Japan and South Korea, foreigners of Asian origin report that they are welcomed much less warmly than Western foreigners. Don't forget what happened in Germany. Welcoming others is the way to stop xenophobia. Let's break down the [3] and learn to love our neighbors.

1. Choose the best answer to complete the missing words in the passage.

1.	2.	3.
(A) fear	(A) empty	(A) interruptions
(B) feared	(B) jealous	(B) locks
(C) fearful	(C) lonely	(C) disturbances
(D) fearless	(D) terrifying	(D) borders

2. Read the passage and choose the best answer to each question.

1. What is the main idea of the article?

    (A) Jewish people stopped the war.

    (B) Anti-foreign feeling causes problems.

    (C) We should complain about neighbors.

    (D) War cannot occur again in Germany.

2. Which group of people did Hitler dislike?

    (A) Jewish.

    (B) Romani.

    (C) Black people.

    (D) All of the above.

**World War II Fact Sheet
Adolf Hitler**

· Leader of the Nazi Party of Germany
· Was taught to dislike Jewish people
· Also strongly hated Romani and Black people
· 6 million Jews were killed during the war
· Hitler shot himself dead in 1945

3. Look at the fact sheet. Which is NOT explained in the article?

    (A) The name of Hitler's political party.

    (B) The groups of people who Hitler disliked.

    (C) The cause of Hitler's death.

    (D) The cause of Hitler's xenophobia.

Reading Tips: *Paraphrasing*

文の内容を自分の言葉で言い換えたりまとめたりする手法は、paraphrasing と呼ばれます。この手法は、剽窃行為 (plagiarism) を防ぎつつ、情報を自分のライティングに取り入れるためにも有効です。以下は、前ページ各段落を言い換えたものです。下線部の単語を本文から書き出しましょう。

1	Xenophobia refers to a d_____ or f_____ of f_____ or unfamiliar people or things. It can be detected in complaints about the presence of f_____ in a c_____ or p_____ l_____ w_____ to foreign workers.
2	Adolf Hitler's hatred towards J_____ people, R_____, and B_____ people stemmed from o____ t_____, which i_____ his l_____ period in Germany.
3	The Nazi party a_____ l_____ in 1935 to discriminate against those people whom H_____ disliked. In the 1940s, the Nazis m_____ many Jewish people, and very few of them s_____.
4	X_____ is still present worldwide, such as cases in S_____ A_____, J_____, and S_____ K_____. We should remember what happened in G_____ and put an end to x_____.

Affirmative action in American universities

In recent years, many elite US universities have been trying to promote ethnic diversity, which would enrich their academic environment. In the US, a policy called **affirmative** action has given advantages to some applicants in certain ethnic groups for college admission. It is aimed at making an active effort to improve educational opportunities for members of
5 minority groups. However, some people refer to it as "**reverse** discrimination." In this essay, the original purpose of **affirmative** action will be introduced, and then discussed from both positive and negative perspectives.

The purpose of **affirmative** action was to **amend** the structural disadvantages of students
10 belonging to minority groups with lower socioeconomic backgrounds (Torres, 2019). In particular, African Americans have had difficulties accessing educational and financial resources caused by racist mistreatment for generations. Therefore, this **affirmative** action was taken as compensation for those who had been historically discriminated against.

15 From the positive perspective, those who stand for this policy expect it to help people to enhance the awareness of their unconscious bias against minority groups "that would otherwise be left unhindered" (Kennedy, 2013, p.11). In 1964, a Civil Rights Act was passed, and some universities started to **allocate** a racial quota. It was one form of **affirmative** action admitting a number of applicants from certain ethnic groups.
20

However, using racial quotas as a form of **affirmative** action was challenged in 1978 in the US Supreme Court. The court decided that quota programs were illegal. This was because the racial quotas may have denied a chance to white applicants. Since then, quota programs have not been widely employed in the US. Moreover, President Obama indicated
25 that he would support class-based **affirmative** action (Shuford, 2009). In this plan, economic circumstances are **taken into account**. Such class-based **affirmative** action is to adequately assist students from lower socioeconomic backgrounds, regardless of their ethnicity.

To conclude, **affirmative** action aims to be a helpful way to solve the problem of
30 racial discrimination in American society. Supporters of this policy argue that it helps raise awareness of unconscious biases and promotes diversity in the academic environment. On the other hand, it can also be a form of **reverse** discrimination. Critics argue that giving advantages to a particular group may cause unfairness among all the groups. Ultimately, the goal is to create inclusive educational environments that provide equal access and support for
35 students from diverse backgrounds. Achieving equal opportunities for all remains an ongoing challenge.

Your Reading Speed: **408** words ÷ _____ seconds × 60 = _____ wpm

References
Kennedy, R. (2013). *For discrimination: race, affirmative action, and the law*. Pantheon Books.
Shuford, R. T. (2009). Why affirmative action remains essential in the age of Obama. *Campbell Law Review, 31*(3), 503–533.
Torres, G. B. (2019). Affirmative action in higher education: Relevance for today's racial justice battlegrounds. *Human Rights Magazine, 44*(4), 6-10.

1. **Choose the phrase that is related to each word / phrase.**

1. affirmative ( )
2. reverse ( )
3. amend ( )
4. allocate ( )
5. take into account ( )

(a) go backwards
(b) positive or effective
(c) to distribute
(d) to fix or improve
(e) to consider

2. **Read the passage and choose the best answer to each question.**

1. What is this essay mainly about?
   (A) Ethnic diversity in the US.
   (B) College tuition in US universities.
   (C) Equal opportunities for college students.
   (D) Application procedures for US universities.

2. Why did affirmative action begin?
   (A) To exclude ethnic minority groups.
   (B) To train students with low ability.
   (C) To pay transportation costs.
   (D) To compensate disadvantaged groups.

3. Choose the appropriate description of quotas.
   (A) Quotas give money to ethnic groups.
   (B) Quotas are seen as affirmative action.
   (C) Quotas provide knowledge about finance.
   (D) Quotas are against the Civil Rights Act.

4. Which of the following did President Obama suggest?
   (A) Having students with similar economic backgrounds study in the same class.
   (B) Having students of the same ethnic group study in the same class.
   (C) Assisting financially disadvantaged students.
   (D) Assisting students of a particular ethnic group.

5. What is the potential downside of affirmative action?
   (A) It doesn't solve the problem of racial discrimination.
   (B) It can benefit all the groups.
   (C) It can lead to reverse discrimination.
   (D) It provides equal opportunities for all.

Writing Tips: *APA (3) When you paraphrase/don't paraphrase*

APA in-text citation は、そのまま文献から言葉を抜き出した場合（direct quote）と、内容を自分の言葉で説明した場合（paraphrase）で表記方法が異なります。70 ページの文章から下の表に対応する in-text citation を書き出しましょう。

In-text citation	Direct quote / Paraphrase
(_____, 2019)	**Paraphrase** The purpose of a_____ a_____ was to amend the structural disadvantages of s_____ b_____ t____ m_____ g_____ with l_____ s_____ b_____
(Kennedy, _____, p. ___)	**Direct quote** "that would o_____ b____ l____ u_____"
(_____, ____).	**Paraphrase** Moreover, P_____ O_____ indicated that he would s_____ c_____ -b_____ a_____ a_____.

Writing Outline: *Citing sources*

Find two sources to explain an organization that promotes diversity. What is the organization? What does each source say about the organization? Paraphrase one, and quote directly from the other.

Introduction	[Organization] is trying to.... I checked some articles and found [**Source 1**], and [**Source 2**].
Source 1	According to [Author (year)].... [Citation]
Source 2	[Author (year)] describes [Organization] as "_____ _____."
Summary	To sum up, [Organization]....
References	

参考文献

Unit 1

OECD (2019). *Education at a glance 2019: OECD indicators*. OECD publishing, Paris. https://doi.org/10.1787/19991487

Unit 2

Howard, R. M. (1992). A plagiarism pentimento. *Journal of Teaching Writing*, *11*(2), 233–45. https://www.scribd.com/doc/220673104/Rebecca-Moore-Howard-A-Plagiarism-Pentimento

Maurer, H. A., Kappe, F., & Zaka, B. (2006). Plagiarism-A survey. *Journal of Universal Computer Science*, *12*(8), 1050–1084. https://www.researchgate.net/publication/220017646_Plagiarism_-_A_Survey

Park, C. (2003). In other (people's) words: Plagiarism by university students—literature and lessons. *Assessment and Evaluation in Higher Education*, *28*(5), 471–488. https://doi.org/10.1080/02602930301677

Unit 3

Drabwell, C.(2018, July 25). *6 tips for teachers on using mobile phones in classrooms*. The Open University. https://ounews.co/education-languages-health/education/6-tips-for-teachers-on-using-mobile-phones-in-classrooms/

Riley, N. S. (2017, February 6). *To fight cyberbullying, ban cellphones from school*. New York Post. https://nypost.com/2017/02/06/to-fight-cyberbullying-ban-cellphones-from-school/

Unit 4

Buchholz, K. (2019, Jun 6). Only three countries in the world (officially) still use the imperial system. Statista. https://www.statista.com/chart/18300/countries-using-the-metric-or-the-imperial-system/

Unit 5

U.S. Bureau of Labor Statistics. (2022, March 31). *May 2021 National Occupational Employment and Wage Estimates*. U.S. Bureau of Labor Statistics. https://www.bls.gov/oes/current/oes_nat.htm

Unit 7

Bombach, A. (Director). (2018). *On her shoulders* [Film]. RYOT Films.

Fayyad, F. (Director). (2017). *Last men in Aleppo* [Film]. Grasshopper Film.

Fazili, H. (Director). (2019). *Midnight traveler* [Film]. Old Chilly Pictures.

Ghaemmaghami, R. (Director). (2015). *Sonita* [Film]. Arte, Norddeutscher Rundfunk (NDR) [de], TAG/TRAUM Filmproduktion.

Pecl, G. T., Araújo, M. B., Bell, J. D., Blanchard, J., Bonebrake, T. C., Chen, I. C., & Williams, S. E. (2017). Biodiversity redistribution under climate change: Impacts on ecosystems and human well-being. *Science*, *355*(6332), 9214.

Sivadas, S. K., Mishra, P., Kaviarasan, T., Sambandam, M., Dhineka, K., Murthy, M. R., & Hoehn, D. (2022). Litter and plastic monitoring in the Indian marine environment: A review of current research, policies, waste management, and a roadmap for multidisciplinary action. *Marine Pollution Bulletin*, *176*, 113424. https://doi.org/10.1016/j.marpolbul.2022.113424

Yue, H., He, C., Huang, Q., Yin, D., & Bryan, B. A. (2020). Stronger policy required to substantially reduce deaths from PM2.5 pollution in China. *Nature Communications*, *11*(1), 1462. https://doi.org/10.1038/s41467-020-15319-4

Unit 8

Statista (2023). *Breakdown of global car sales in 2019 and 2030, by fuel technology*. https://www.statista.com/statistics/827460/global-car-sales-by-fuel-technology/

United States Department of Transportation (n.d.). *Automated Driving Systems*. National Highway Traffic Safety Administration. https://www.nhtsa.gov/vehicle-manufacturers/automated-driving-systems

Unit 9

Helliwell, J. F., Layard, R., Sachs, J. D., De Neve, J. E., Aknin, L. B., & Wang, S. (Eds.). (2022). *World Happiness Report 2022*. Sustainable Development Solutions Network.

Unit 10

Bosley, S., & Knorr, M. (2018). Pyramids, Ponzis and fraud prevention: Lessons from a case study. *Journal of Financial Crime*, *25* (1), 81–94. https://doi.org/10.1108/JFC-10-2016-0062

Unit 11

National Health Service. (2023). *When to go to A&E*. https://www.nhs.uk/nhs-services/urgent-and-emergency-care-services/when-to-go-to-ae/

Unit 12

Kennedy, R. (2013). *For discrimination: race, affirmative action, and the law*. Pantheon Books.

Shuford, R. T. (2009). Why affirmative action remains essential in the age of Obama. *Campbell Law Review*, *31*(3), 503–533.

Torres, G. B. (2019). Affirmative action in higher education: Relevance for today's racial justice battlegrounds. *Human Rights Magazine*, *44*(4), 6-10.

TEXT PRODUCTION STAFF

| edited by | 編集 |
| Hiroko Nakazawa | 中澤 ひろ子 |

| English-language editing by | 英文校正 |
| Bill Benfield | ビル・ベンフィールド |

| cover design by | 表紙デザイン |
| Nobuyoshi Fujino | 藤野 伸芳 |

| text design by | 本文デザイン |
| Nobuyoshi Fujino | 藤野 伸芳 |

CD PRODUCTION STAFF

narrated by	吹き込み者
Dominic Allen (American English)	ドミニク・アレン（アメリカ英語）
Jack Merluzzi (American English)	ジャック・マルジ（アメリカ英語）
Jennifer Okano (American English)	ジェニファー・オカノ（アメリカ英語）
Karen Hedrick (American English)	カレン・ヘドリック（アメリカ英語）

Global Perspectives
Reading & Writing Book 1

2024年1月20日　初版発行
2024年2月15日　第2刷発行

編著者　中西 のりこ　Nicholas Musty　大竹 翔子

Tam Shuet Ying　Mary Ellis

発行者　佐野 英一郎

発行所　株式会社 成 美 堂
〒101-0052 東京都千代田区神田小川町 3-22
TEL 03-3291-2261　　FAX 03-3293-5490
http://www.seibido.co.jp

印刷・製本　（株）倉敷印刷

ISBN 978-4-7919-7284-5　　　　　　　　　　　　　　Printed in Japan